PHIL GORDON'S

LITTLE GREEN

BOOK

PHIL GORDON'S

LITTLE GREEN

BOOK

Lessons and Teachings in
No Limit Texas Hold'em

by Phil Gordon

SIMON SPOTLIGHT ENTERTAINMENT
New York London Toronto Sydney

Poker is a wonderful game that can be incredibly rewarding to play, but for some, gambling can become an unhealthy addiction. If you believe that you or someone you know is a compulsive gambler, you should contact Gambler's Anonymous at www.gamblersanonymous.org and seek professional help immediately. Also, if you're playing for cash, you should know that gambling for money is illegal in some countries, states, and cities, so before you gamble for money, check the laws in your local jurisdiction.

SᏚᎬ

SIMON SPOTLIGHT ENTERTAINMENT

An imprint of Simon & Schuster

1230 Avenue of the Americas, New York, New York 10020

Copyright © 2005 by Phil Gordon

All rights reserved, including the right of reproduction in whole or in part in any form.

SIMON SPOTLIGHT ENTERTAINMENT and related logo are trademarks of Simon & Schuster, Inc.

Book design by Yaffa Jaskoll

Manufactured in the United States of America

20 19 18 17 16 15 14

Library of Congress Cataloging-in-Publication Data

Gordon, Phil–, 1970–

[Little Green Book]

Phil Gordon's little green book : lessons and teachings in no limit Texas hold'em / by Phil Gordon ; foreword by Howard Lederer and Annie Duke—1st ed.

p. cm.

Includes bibliographical references and index.

ISBN-13: 978-1-4169-0367-3

ISBN-10: 1-4169-0367-4

1. Poker I. Title.

GV1251.G66 2005   795.412—dc22   2005010872

DEDICATION

To the three women in my life who have always been there for me and taught me everything I need to know to be a winner—my mom, Ann, my little sister, Ashley, and my dear aunt, Marie "Lib" Elizabeth Lucas. My first poker game was with these three ladies. They busted me.

CONTENTS

Foreword by Howard Lederer and Annie Duke   xv

Acknowledgments   xix

Introduction   1

Poker Truths   5

    Decisions, Decisions   6

    Consequences   6

    Getting It In with the Best Hand   7

    The Fundamental Theorem   8

    It's My Turn to Bet. . . . Think!   9

    I Don't Have to Be the Greatest   11

    Common Mistakes   12

Observing My Opponents   14

Value of Aggression   16

Position, Position, Position   16

Money Flows Clockwise   17

Blinds Have a Negative Expectation   18

Have a Reason to Bet   19

Changing Gears   20

Learn from Better Players   21

Big Hand Big Pot, Small Hand Small Pot   22

Before the Flop   23

Study, Then Look   26

When First in the Pot, Raise   26

Limping   28

Raise the Right Amount   31

Calling Limpers   32

In Position, Smooth-Call a Raiser   34

Playing from the Small Blind   36

Raising from the Big Blind   39

Raise the Limpers   40

The Chip-Sandwich Play   41

Steal from the Cutoff   43

Preflop Domination   44

Playing Great Hands When They Raise   46

All-in Before the Flop   49

The Fourth Raise Means Aces   50

Know When a Player Is Pot Committed   52

Re-raise to Isolate   52

Pocket Pairs in Multiway Pots   54

After the Flop   56

First to the Pot Wins   58

Heads-Up Postflop   59

Against Multiple Opponents   65

Betting to Slow Down an Opponent   68

Double Gut-Shot Straight Draws   69

Hands to Bring to War   70

Board Texture   72

Bet Good Hands   74

After Flopping Two Pair   75

After Flopping a Set   79

After Flopping Trips   82

After Flopping a Straight   85

After Flopping a Flush   89

After Flopping a Full House   91

After Flopping Four of a Kind   94

After Flopping a Draw   95

When I Bet and a Good Player Calls   98

After the Turn   99

When I Improve My Hand   101

When a Scare Card Hits   104

Calling with a Draw   105

Semibluffing 106

Taking Down the Pot 108

After the River 110

Getting Paid with the Nuts 112

Betting Medium-Strength Hands 113

Bet or Check-Raise 116

Tells 118

Caro's Great Law of Tells 120

Beware of the Speech 120

Varied Bet Sizes 122

The Out-of-Turn Bet 122

Big Chips, Small Chips 124

Chip Stacks 125

When They're Busy, They're Tight 127

Suit Check 128

Quick Bet, Slow Bet 128

Changes in Demeanor 129

Leaners and Slouchers 129

Shaky Hands 130

When They Look at Their Chips 131

When They Look at My Chips 131

The Quick Call 132

The Slow Call 132

When They Reach for Their Chips 133

Toss vs. Slide 133

Reverse Tells   134

Tournament Strategies   136

     Staying Alive   138

     Build a Tight Image Early   138

     When the Pot Is Big   139

     Take a Time-Out After Significant Changes   139

     Know Their Stack Size   141

     Get Lucky . . . at the Right Time   141

     Target the Average Stacks   142

     Play Small Pocket Pairs   143

     Don't Go Broke with One Pair   144

     Sample Tournament Payout Structure   145

     Playing to Win Tournaments   147

     Money Means Something   148

     Making a Deal   149

     Steal the Blinds!   150

     When Stealing the Blinds Doesn't Work   153

     Steal or Re-raise?   155

     Keep the Average Stack Size in Mind   156

     Be Comfortable at Thirty Big Bets   157

     Playing the Big Stack   158

     When the Antes Start   162

     Short Stacks   162

     Super Short Stack Strategy   163

     Wait for the Blinds to Increase   166

Rebuys and Add-Ons 167

Bubbles 168

Last Hand Before a Break 169

Implicit Collusion Late in a Tournament 170

Sobering Math and Bad Beats 172

Some Percentages and Math 176

The Rules of Four and Two 178

A-K, A-A, K-K 180

The Value of Suitedness 181

Preflop Matchups 182

Slight Dog, Big Favorite 184

Interesting, Unexpected Matchups 184

Pot Odds and Implied Odds 186

Psychology 192

Big Laydowns 194

Bury Them 198

After a Bad Beat 199

Superstitions 200

Rushes 201

Watch for Betting Patterns 202

Beating Tight and Passive Players 203

Beating Loose Players 204

Beating Calling Stations 205

Beating Overly Aggressive Opponents 206

When to Change Gears 207

Seat Selection 209

Forming a Game Plan 209

Showing My Cards 211

Tilt 211

Implied Tilt Odds 214

Game Selection 214

Timing of Bets 215

Bluffing 216

Making the Big Bluff 216

Miscellaneous 222

Stakes and Bankroll 223

Session Length 224

Stop-Loss or Win Goals 225

Advance Scouting 226

Chopping the Blinds 226

Don't Tap on the Aquarium 227

Practice Makes Perfect 228

Sick Gamblers 229

Sunglasses at the Table 230

Staking and Getting Staked 231

Aggression Is the Great Equalizer 232

Tournament Structures 233

Online Poker 235

Player Profiles 238

Gus Hansen 239

Dan Harrington   241
Phil Hellmuth Jr.   242
Chris "Jesus" Ferguson   243
Howard Lederer   244
John Juanda   245
"Biggest Online Winner"   245
Rules of No Limit Hold'em   250
The Basics   250
Rules of Etiquette   257
Tournament Rules and Procedures   259
Charts and Tables   260
Starting Hands   261
Outs   270
Preflop Chances   271
Hand Rankings   274
WSOP Tournament Structure   276
FullTiltPoker.com Sit & Go
Tournament Structure   277
Further Study   278
Books   278
Periodicals   280
Web sites   281
Shameless Plugs   282
Afterword   284

FOREWORD

By Howard Lederer and Annie Duke

We have both known Phil Gordon for many years. We have known what a smart man he is—it takes a brilliant mind to become an Internet whiz kid just out of college. We have known him as a *World Series of Poker* (*WSOP*) championship event finalist and a *World Poker Tour* (*WPT*) champion. We have known him as the insightful host of Bravo's *Celebrity Poker Showdown* (*CPS*). We have known him as a friend. But what we did not know until he passed his manuscript on to us is that this man can write a damn good poker book.

What Phil offers you here, dear reader, is an experience unique in the world of poker literature. Other poker books offer the important and necessary foundation that will help you understand the statistics and probability involved in the game. These books also offer general strategic advice and starting-hand charts. Phil offers you all of that as well. But Phil took the next step and raised the bar. He also offers a look into the mind and thought processes of a great player.

Books on the foundation of poker should be devoured. No one has ever become a great player without having a basic understanding of probability theory and game theory. Chew that information up. Digest it. Spit it out.

This book, however, should be sipped and savored like a good meal or a great bottle of wine. Read it slowly. Take the time to truly grasp and appreciate what Phil is saying. There isn't another book out there that will get you inside the mind of a great player so deeply and incisively.

When we were starting out, we learned quickly that all the general strategic advice on earth only gets you so far in the game. What really got us to where we are today is talking: talking to each other about situations and hands we had played and talking to pros about the same thing. To become a great player you need to open your mind to the thought processes of great thinkers and players. You need to always be willing to consider other people's opinions about why and how a hand should be played.

Poker is a game of incomplete information—correct decision-making depends on many, many factors. Playing perfectly is never attainable. All we can do as players is strive to make the best decisions we can under uncertain circumstances, always having the goal of that perfect session in mind.

What keeps us alive and growing as players is the constant questioning of what we do and how we make our decisions. *Phil Gordon's Little Green Book* is a guidebook to the kind of critical thinking that will keep you improving as a player. Instead of offering dry and general strategic advice, he offers you insight into how he thinks. You may, in the end, reject some of his conclusions as not a good stylistic fit for you. But this is exactly what Phil wants from you. He offers here deep insight into how he plays, how he thinks. He is not telling you how you should play. We hope that you will incorporate some of what he does into your game, because we know he does most things brilliantly.

But even the principles you reject will make you a better player. One thing this book will teach you is that everything you do at the poker table needs to have a reason—there needs to be a well thought-out process behind each play. If you reject a strategy from this book, we hope that you reject it with good reason. (You have probably rejected or accepted other strategic advice from other poker books or players before.) After reading this book, you will make decisions with a deeper understanding of why, and a more advanced awareness of the critical thought processes in your game.

So read this book slowly. Read it more than once. As you improve, keep looking back at what Phil has to say, because every time you do, you will learn something new. We have been playing this game for a very long time. We have reached the top of the game. And yet we both came away better players and thinkers for having read this book. We thank you, Phil, for opening up your game in such an honest and forthcoming way.

In our minds this book is an instant classic and a must-have for any serious student of the game. Everyone who reads it will come away a better player.

ACKNOWLEDGMENTS

I would like to thank all the Tiltboys (Rafe Furst, Dave "Diceboy" Lambert, Steve Miranda, Perry Friedman, Paul Swiencicki, Tony Glenning, Kim Scheinberg, John Kullmann, Josh Paley, Michael Stern, Lenny Augustine, Bruce Hayek, Russ Garber) for fifteen years of poker fun. Wednesday night, Tiltboy Poker Night, is still the best night of the week. The games of "Spit-and-Shit Ding-a-Ling-with-a-Twist" will always be among my favorite poker memories.

I'd like to also thank my family and friends for their love and support. Much love to Mom, Dad, sister

Ashley, brother-in-law Ryan, nephew Zakai and niece Anise, Barb Smith, Rick Averitt, godchildren Quinn and Savannah Averitt, Ben Philip Leader, and Winnie and Charlie Swiencicki.

In business you need people whom you can trust. I am very lucky to have some incredibly talented people on my side: my agents, Andy Elkin, Lisa Shotland, Amy Yavor, and Jeremy Plager at Creative Artists Agency; my PR guy, Jeff Duclos; and my literary agents, Greg Dinkin and Frank Scatoni of Venture Literary. Thanks to my friends and business partners at P3 Poker, PJ O'Neill, Luke Lincoln, and Brian Efird. Thanks to Brian "Gio" Smith of HighRoller Fashions. Thank you to the kind folks at NTN—playing poker in bars has never been more fun. Without the assistance of my assistant Dorian Dianni, I'd never get anything done. Thanks to the folks at Simon Spotlight Entertainment who believed in me and this project: Tricia Boczkowski, Jen Bergstrom, Jen Robinson, Jen Slattery, Julie Amitie, Nellie Kurtzman, Lynn Smith, Suzanne Murphy, Rick Richter, Russell Gordon, Yaffa Jaskoll, Emily Westlake, Bill Gaden, and Frank Fochetta.

In every poker player's life there are people who bring you along, share their knowledge, secrets, and experiences. My friends at FullTiltPoker.com are without a doubt the best players in the world. Their tutelage and friendship are, in large part, responsible for my success in poker. Chris "Jesus" Ferguson, Howard Lederer, Phil Ivey, John Juanda, Erik Seidel, Erick Lindgren, Jennifer Harman, Clonie Gowen, and Andy Bloch are always willing to talk about hands, rejoice in successes, and sympathize with bad beats. Many of these incredibly talented players have read through this book and suggested corrections and improvements.

Special thanks to my friends who took an extraordinary amount of time to help edit this book: Jonathan Grotenstein, Richard "Quiet Lion" Brody, Rick "J-2" Wampler, Annie Duke, Andrew Hill Newman, Richard Lederer, Mike Keller, and Jon Gunn.

Finally, thanks to my friends from Bravo's *Celebrity Poker Showdown*: Dave Foley, Andrew Hill Newman, and Josh Malina; the rest of the *CPS* crew; Picture This Television; and the many celebrities who come to play a little Texas Hold'em for charity.

My great-aunt Lib Lucas taught me to play poker when I was seven. She died of cancer the day I won my first major poker tournament. Every hand I play and tournament I enter I dedicate to her. A portion of the proceeds from this book will be donated to the Cancer Research and Prevention Foundation (www.preventcancer.org) in her memory.

Fortune favors the prepared mind.
—Louis Pasteur

PHIL GORDON'S
LITTLE GREEN
BOOK

INTRODUCTION

No Limit Hold'em is a very tough game. That's the bad news. But here is some good news: You can learn. How do I know you can learn? Because I was not always a winning player, and I learned. If I can go from "dead money" to *World Poker Tour* champion, there is no doubt that others can as well.

The greatest poker players in the world share five qualities:

1. They are invariably aggressive. Aggressive poker is winning poker. They apply pressure to their opponents with bets and raises.

2. They are patient. They wait for situations at the table that are profitable.
3. They are courageous. They don't need the stone-cold nuts to bet, call, or raise.
4. They are observant. They watch their opponents during every hand.
5. They are always working on their game and want to be even better players. They talk about the game with other players. They practice. They read poker books. They analyze their play and work to plug "leaks" that have developed.

These five qualities are all that are necessary to be a great, winning player. The first four qualities you can learn and develop. You already have the fifth quality—you bought this book so you're working on your game.

There are many ways to win at this game. I intend in this book to write exactly how I play. You may disagree with many of the plays that I recommend here. Good. I want you to approach this book not as a definitive guide for how to play, but as a catalyst for thinking about the game.

In short, the following pages are, to the best of my ability, how I play No Limit Texas Hold'em. I'm not the best player in the world. But I'm a winning player, and I win playing exactly the style that is described here.

Throughout my poker education I have read nearly every book on poker ever written. I owe a great deal to the poker authors that have come before me. Sklansky. Brunson. Cloutier. McEvoy. Malmuth. Cooke. Harrington. Caro. Without their work I wouldn't be the player that I am today. Most of the things I know about the game I owe to these authors.

Harvey Penick, arguably the greatest golf teacher that ever lived, wrote a great book, *Harvey Penick's Little Red Book*. In that book he recorded his thoughts and musings on the game of golf. Not once in his book did he profess to know the only way to play. I drew inspiration from Mr. Penick's book and his straightforward approach to teaching a very difficult game.

Take your time with this book. No matter how thoroughly you digest the contents, you'll need to play thousands of hands against all kinds of competition before things will really "click" for you. Take your time. Your bankroll will not be built overnight. Grow it slowly. There will be setbacks. There will be bad beats. But, there will be endless amounts of joy as your game improves.

POKER TRUTHS

You have chosen a tough game. As talented professional and *World Poker Tour* host Mike Sexton is fond of saying, "No Limit Texas Hold'em takes a minute to learn and a lifetime to master."

There are many different ways to win and many different styles of play. But regardless of the path you take, there are a few universally accepted axioms, "poker truths," that apply to the game no matter how it is played. In this section I present some of the truths that I've learned, discovered, or been taught over the years.

DECISIONS, DECISIONS

Winning poker is not about winning money. Nor is it about reading tells or being the best bluffer. It's not about winning the most pots. *Winning poker is about making correct decisions.*

In every hand I play, I am faced with many important decisions:

♣ Should I play this hand?
♣ How much should I raise?
♣ Do I have the best hand?
♣ Can I get my opponent to fold?

If I make better decisions more often than my opponents, I will win. I may not win the most pots. But I will win, and win consistently.

CONSEQUENCES

While seated at the poker table, every action—or inaction—has consequences. My goal is to master my own behavior while manipulating the behavior of my opponents. With every check, bet, raise, or fold, I am trying to minimize the consequences of *my* mistakes and maximize the consequences of *their* mistakes.

GETTING IT IN WITH THE BEST HAND

All I can do is get my money in the pot with the best hand. No matter how hard I try, I can't control the cards after the money is in the pot. All I can do is get my money—as much money as possible—into the pot when I have the best hand.

Bad beats, suckouts, and lucky catches for my opponents are an essential part of the game. If bad players couldn't occasionally get lucky and win, there would be no poker games worth playing.

It does me no good whatsoever to fret about losing a pot if I got my money into the pot with the best hand.

THE FUNDAMENTAL THEOREM

In his groundbreaking book, *The Theory of Poker*, David Sklansky writes:

> Every time you play a hand differently from the way you would have played it if you could see all your opponents' cards, they gain; and every time you play your hand the same way you would have played it if you could see all their cards, they lose. Conversely, every time opponents play their hands differently from the way they would have if they could see all your cards, they lose; and every time they play their hands the same way they would have played if they could see all your cards, you lose.

If I could somehow know my opponents' hole cards, there would be a right and a wrong decision to make at every step along the way: I should be betting or raising when I have the best hand, checking or folding when I have the worst hand, and calling when I have the right pot odds or implied odds to see another card. I should be maximizing the money my opponents put into the pot when I have the best hand and minimizing the money I put in when I have the worst hand.

The Fundamental Theorem is simple, but poker is not a simple game. I don't often know my opponents' hole cards. To be a great player I have to combine the principles of The Fundamental Theorem with the many psychological considerations that are part of the game.

IT'S MY TURN TO BET. . . . THINK!

Every single time it's my turn to act, I try to run a simple script through my head:

♥ How are my opponents playing? Conservatively? Aggressively? Tentatively?
♥ What are some of the hands my opponents are likely to hold?
♥ What do my opponents think I have?
♥ Am I in good position or bad position?

After processing the answers to those questions, I move on to the most important questions:

♠ Should I bet (or raise)?

- If I think I have the best hand, I nearly always answer yes, and I bet or raise.
- If I think I can force weak opponents out of the pot with this bet or with future bets, I nearly always answer yes, and I bet or raise.
- If I have a good draw and I think there is a good chance that my opponents will fold, I nearly always answer yes, and I bet or raise.

♠ Should I check (or fold)?

- If I think I have the worst hand, I nearly always answer yes, and I check or fold.
- If I think my opponents are strong, I nearly always answer yes, and I check or fold.
- If I'm on a draw but not getting a good price, I nearly always answer yes, and I check or fold.

If, after careful analysis, I don't think I should raise and I don't think I should fold, I feel confident that calling a bet (or checking) is correct.

I have found that running this script through my head, even in seemingly straightforward or obvious situations, will often allow me to identify opportunities that other players might miss.

By asking the bet-or-raise question before the

check-or-fold question, I ensure that I am playing aggressive poker. Aggressive poker is winning poker.

I DON'T HAVE TO BE THE GREATEST

I don't have to be the best player at the table. All I have to do to win is play better than a few of my opponents.

Most of the money passed around the table will come from two or three bad players. I will do my best to get the money from the players who are weaker than I am and to keep my money away from the players who are stronger.

In March 2003, just after the *World Poker Tour* started airing, throngs of tourists with big money flocked to Las Vegas, chomping at the bit to play No Limit Hold'em. One night at the Bellagio, I passed by a No Limit game with $10 and $20 blinds. Seated at the table were Antonio Esfandiari, Gus Hansen, Phil Laak, Rafe Furst, and maybe three other name players.

I couldn't imagine why any one of them would be in the game. None of the pros had a huge edge over any of the others. I certainly didn't consider myself a favorite against this lineup.

And then I saw the weak spot. "Harry" was a true angel from Austin, Texas. He had wads of hundreds, banded in $10,000 bundles, and he was betting at least one of them on what seemed like every single hand.

There was a seat open. I took it.

COMMON MISTAKES

Everyone makes mistakes. A bad player will make the same mistake over and over again. Poker players who can exploit these mistakes will win. Here are some of the most common mistakes that bad players make, and my usual methods for exploiting them:

♦ **A player doesn't bluff enough.** When these players bet or raise, I usually give them credit for a good hand. When they check, I will usually bet to try to take the pot.
♦ **A player overvalues top pair.** The average winning hand in Hold'em is two pair. Yet many players are willing to take tremendous risks with top pair. When I have a hand that can beat a player who overvalues their top

pair, I will overbet the pot and put them into a position to make a big mistake. I go out of my way to play small pocket pairs against these players because I know that if I flop a set, I'm likely to get paid off in a huge way. (See "Pot Odds and Implied Odds," page 186.)

♦ **A player underbets the pot.** It is incredibly important, especially in No Limit Hold'em, to make bets large enough to punish opponents for their draws. (See "Pot Odds and Implied Odds," page 186.) When a player underbets the pot and I have a draw, I take advantage of their mistake by just calling the small bet. When I think I have them beat, I'll make a raise.

♦ **A player calls too much.** I will very rarely bluff against a "calling station." I will, however, make value bets throughout the hand.

♦ **A player tightens up under pressure.** Most bad players "squeeze" too much in the middle stages of a tournament, or when they're on the bubble. They tighten up and wait for a huge hand. Against these players, I will play a lot looser, looking to steal a larger share of the blinds and antes.

♦ **A player telegraphs the strength of his hand with "tells."** I am always observing these players, whether I am in the hand or not. (See "Tells," page 118.)

> He who can modify his tactics in relation to
> his opponent and thereby succeed in winning
> may be called a heaven-born captain.
> —Sun Tzu, *The Art of War*

OBSERVING MY OPPONENTS

One of the best things I can do to increase my chances of winning is to constantly observe my opponents, even when I am not in the hand.

♣ I look for tells.
♣ I look for betting patterns.
♣ I try to put my opponents on hands.
♣ If my opponent shows down a hand, I remember their cards, their position, and what they did with that hand before the flop and after the flop.
♣ I try to figure out what state of mind my opponents are in.
♣ I think about what is motivating them.

The more I observe my opponents, the more information I have to draw on when I actually get into a pot with them.

The most valuable example of observation I've ever seen occurred at the final table of the *World Series of Poker* in 2001. We were down to five players when Phil Hellmuth Jr. and Carlos Mortensen tangled in what turned out to be a very important hand. The flop had come Q-9-4 with two spades, and Carlos, after a $60,000 bet from Phil, decided to check-raise to $200,000. Phil immediately moved all-in for about $400,000.

Carlos, who had Q-J, had him covered but clearly feared that Phil had flopped a huge hand. As Carlos debated his move, muttering under his breath, Phil thought he heard the word "call" and—for just a brief second—exposed his hand: Q-T. The *observant* Carlos called instantly and, when the turn and river failed to improve either of their hands, he busted Phil Hellmuth Jr. out of the tournament in fifth place. The crowd, with the exception of Phil's wife and parents, cheered wildly.

VALUE OF AGGRESSION

When I check or call, the only way I will win is if I have the best hand at the showdown.

When I bet or raise, I have *two ways* to win: My opponent may fold *or* I may have the best hand at the showdown.

The players I fear most at the table are the players who consistently bet and raise. Checkers and callers usually don't last very long.

POSITION, POSITION, POSITION

Having good position (being last to act on every round of betting) in No Limit Hold'em is extremely important for several reasons:

♥ I get to see what all of my opponents do before I have to decide if I am going to commit any chips to the pot.
♥ I have the last chance to bluff.
♥ I can take advantage of the difficulty of flopping a

good hand. In Texas Hold'em an opponent with unpaired hole cards (A-K, K-Q, 6-4, etc.) will only flop a pair or better about 35% of the time. When they miss the other 65% of the time, my position will allow me to take advantage regardless of the strength of my hand.

♥ When I am in position, it is infinitely easier to extract the most money possible from opponents who have a good hand—but not the best hand.

I'd estimate that for 75–80% of the hands I get involved in, I am playing from superior position. Against strong opponents, I will *very rarely* play a hand from out of position.

MONEY FLOWS CLOCKWISE

Because of the many advantages of playing a hand from good position, money at the poker table tends to flow in a clockwise direction, away from the blinds and toward the players who are last to act.

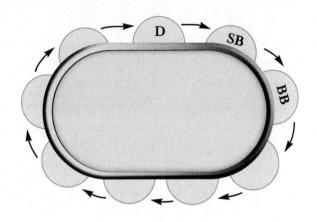

BLINDS HAVE A NEGATIVE EXPECTATION

I expect, over the long term, to lose money on the hands I play from the blinds. I don't really worry about it so much, since there will be plenty of opportunities to make back my blinds (and more) when I'm playing in position.

The blinds have a negative expectation primarily because they are first to act on every round of betting after the flop. The hands that I've had the most success playing from out of position are small and medium pocket pairs. Flopping a set is a great way to win a big pot from any position.

HAVE A REASON TO BET

When I'm putting chips into the pot, I always have a good reason to do so. Here are some of the reasons I put chips into the pot before the flop:

♠ To steal the blinds. (See "Steal the Blinds!" page 150.)
♠ To isolate a player when I'm in better position. (See "Re-raise to Isolate," page 52.)
♠ Because I think I have the best hand.
♠ To set up a delayed steal—I call from position and after my opponent misses the flop, I intend to take the pot.
♠ Because I think if I make a hand, my opponents will pay me off in a big way. (See "Pot Odds and Implied Odds," page 186.)

Here are some of the reasons I put chips into the pot after the flop:

♦ I think there is a reasonable chance my opponent will fold.
♦ I think my opponent has a draw, and I want to either make them pay for the privilege of drawing or make them fold a hand that can catch up.

♦ I think I have the best hand.
♦ Betting is the only chance I have to win the pot.
♦ I know I have the best hand, and I want my opponents to put chips into the pot.

CHANGING GEARS

It is very easy to beat players who always play the same way. If they're tight, I will fold when they finally decide to enter a pot, or I will force them out of pots with unrelenting steal attempts. If they're very loose, I try to play tight and wait for good cards. If they always bet straight or flush draws on the flop, I tend to raise their bets on the flop more often than usual.

The point is this: When my opponents are predictable, I very rarely make a big mistake against them. More important, I can use the knowledge I have about them to force them to make big mistakes.

Being able to "change gears" is one of the most important attributes a winning player possesses. Sometimes it is right to play tight. Sometimes it is right to play loose. But it is *always* right to keep my opponents guessing as to what mode I'm in by changing from one gear to the next.

In battle, there are not more than two methods of attack—the direct and the indirect; yet these two in combination give rise to an endless series of maneuvers.
—Sun Tzu, *The Art of War*

LEARN FROM BETTER PLAYERS

There are many people in the game who are better players than I am. Rather than feeling intimidated, I make a conscious effort to learn from them. Each and every time I play with a player who is better than I am, it is an opportunity to learn and improve my own game.

BIG HAND BIG POT, SMALL HAND SMALL POT

It may seem obvious, but when I have a big hand, I try to play a very big pot. When I have a small hand, I try to play a small pot. When an opponent is looking to build a big pot by making a large raise, I am willing to throw away most of my smaller hands so that I have a better chance of sticking around long enough to get into a big pot with a big hand. I will rarely play a big pot without a big hand.

BEFORE THE FLOP

Once I am involved in a hand, many of the actions I take after the flop are automatic, or nearly automatic. Therefore, the most important decisions in No Limit Hold'em take place before the flop: Should I play the two cards I've been dealt?

Many factors come into play in answering this question. Most poker texts offer a chart that tells what two cards to play from each position. I offer my own version later in the book (see "Starting Hands," page 261), but with the following disclaimer: Poker is not a game that is best played by the numbers. Poker is a game of *situations.*

In blackjack there is always a correct decision to be made, what players call "basic strategy." Once you have compared the strength of your hand against the dealer's up card, the odds will—or at least *should*—dictate whether it's best to hit, stand, split, and so on.

Poker, however, is a game of incomplete information and is therefore much more complex. There are many factors to consider that go above and beyond what "the book" says to do. Some of them include:

♣ My opponents' tendencies
♣ Our states of mind
♣ Our stack sizes
♣ My image at the table

Computer programs can look up hands in a chart. Real poker players analyze situations and make their own decisions after processing all the information. I might raise with A-J from early position in one game and fold the same hand from the same position in another.

The starting hand requirements I offer in the tables near the end of this book closely approximate the way I will play under the following *very specific set of circumstances*:

♥ I am the first person to voluntarily put money into the pot and am going to come in for a raise of about three times the big blind.

♥ I don't know much about my opponents.

♥ All the players at the table have an average-size stack.

♥ The blinds are relatively small in relation to the size of the stacks.

If you're a new player, these tables are a great place to start. The more poker you play, however, the more comfortable you will feel letting your experience, your instincts, and, of course, the concepts that follow serve as your guide.

STUDY, THEN LOOK

I never look at my cards before it is my turn to act. I find that if I look at my hand as soon as the cards are dealt, I am often uninterested in the action if I have a bad hand and overly interested if I have a good hand. Players who are paying attention can easily pick up this tell and use it against me when deciding if they should play their hands.

Waiting until it's my turn to act before looking at my cards also helps me to stay focused on what everyone else is doing. By concentrating on how each opponent acts before the flop, I often pick up valuable information that helps me later in the hand and in the game.

WHEN FIRST IN THE POT, RAISE

I very rarely limp (just call the big blind) when I am the first player to voluntarily put chips into the pot before the flop. If I decide to play my hand and I am the first person in, I almost always raise. Here are five reasons why:

♠ **To limit the competition.** A raise will almost always result in fewer players seeing the flop. Fewer players means that I have a better chance of winning with my hand.

- Pocket aces against a random hand wins 85.5% of the time. Pocket aces against four random hands wins 55.8% of the time.
- A hand played against a single opponent is much easier to analyze and play than a hand played against multiple opponents.

♠ **To take control of the betting.** By raising before the flop, I am informing the other players that I have a high expectation of winning this pot. Any postflop bets I make will back up my initial portrayal of strength. I become the table captain for this hand, and if my opponents want to try to win the pot, they are going to have to take it away from me.

"Check to the raiser" is a phrase I've heard many times when playing in home games. That is exactly the mentality I want my opponents to have when I raise before the flop.

♠ **To better define my opponents' hands.** Let's say I limp in before the flop and the big blind just checks. He could literally have any two cards.

- Did he check a strong hand like K-Q?
- Does he have 7-2?
- Maybe he was dealt 3-3.

But if I raise before the flop and get called, I can at least eliminate, with some confidence, the worst third or half of my opponents' potential hands.

♠ **To make it more difficult for my opponents to determine the strength of my hand.** Players who only raise with their premium hands and limp in with their suited connectors and small pocket pairs are giving away too much information. Once I identify a player who uses this tactic, I will almost always raise when they limp in, as most of the time they are going to fold.

If I raise with 6-5 suited and with A-A, I very effectively conceal the strength of my hand.

♠ **To win the blinds.** My opening raise will always give me a chance to *win*—or *steal*—the blinds without having to see the flop. I love stealing the blinds! I make a living by stealing the blinds. Stealing the blinds is critical to my success in tournament poker.

LIMPING

While I'm generally not a big fan of limping into a pot for the reasons I've just described, there are many great players who limp a lot and have spectacular success with this tactic. Daniel Negreanu, Gus Hansen, and Erick Lindgren are good examples of world-class players who limp quite often. As I have said many times, there is more than one way to be a winning poker player.

I can think of several situations where limping *might* be preferable to raising before the flop:

♦ **I have a very strong hand and suspect that a player behind me may raise if I limp.** When I'm sitting at a table with maniacs who are raising every time, or against short stacks looking for a chance to push all of their chips into the middle, this can be a very effective strategy.

♦ **The players in the blinds are weak after the flop.** If I know I can outplay opponents after the flop, it sometimes makes sense to keep them in the hand long enough for them to make a big mistake. For example, I might limp in from middle or late position against a player in the blind who consistently overbets the pot after the flop. I give up a small amount of preflop expectation for some excellent implied odds after the flop. (See "Pot Odds and Implied Odds," page 186.)

♦ **Limping will help me deceive my opponents.** By occasionally limping in with a very good hand, I may be able to train my opponents to allow me to limp in with marginal hands. A player burned by this strategy will be less likely to re-raise me the next time I limp in.

I have found limping to be most effective when I do it with a marginal hand about four times more often than I do with big hands. Why is that? Mathematics.

Assume my opponents are likely to raise about five times the size of the big blind when I limp, in an effort to get me to fold. If I follow the four to one ratio above, then four out of five times I will have a mediocre hand that I will have to fold after my opponents raise. Over the course of those hands I will lose the equivalent of four big blinds. On the fifth time, however, I will have a strong hand, re-raise the raiser, and (hopefully) win the pot right there. I will win the money they have raised—about five times the size of the big blind—and cover the four times I have lost, leaving me with a net gain equivalent to one big blind.

20%	20%	20%	20%	20%
Limp,	Limp,	Limp,	Limp,	Limp,
Fold	Fold	Fold	Fold	Re-raise
Lose 1	Lose 1	Lose 1	Lose 1	Win 5

Net = +1

RAISE THE RIGHT AMOUNT

If I'm the first to voluntarily commit chips to the pot before the flop, I nearly always raise. In my early days I would raise about three times the big blind, a practice I still suggest to every new player. As my skills have increased, I have found a pattern of raising that works much better for me than the standard three-times multiplier:

My Position	Raise
Early	2.5x–3.0x
Middle	3.0x–3.5x
Late	3.5x–4.0x
Small blind	3.0x

There are several reasons why I vary my raise according to position:

♣ I commit fewer chips to the pot when I am out of position.

♣ A smaller raise from early position encourages opponents to play against me when I have a powerhouse hand.

♣ Bigger raises from late position put real pressure on

the remaining players to fold and make it harder for the blinds to re-raise.

♣ When I'm playing in position, there is more money in the pot.

I *do not* vary the size of my raise with the strength of my hand. Raising by the same multiplier every time prevents my opponents from defining my hand by the size of my bet. They won't know whether I'm raising with J-8 suited hoping to steal the blinds or with pocket aces praying for action.

Raising before the flop is designed, in part, to limit the competition. If I find that a raise of three times the big blind is ineffective and that many opponents are still calling my preflop raise, I tighten up my starting hand requirements and I raise much more than three times the big blind. I've played in games where a standard preflop raise was almost ten times the blind.

CALLING LIMPERS

While I don't like to be the first player to limp into a pot, I am more than happy to call limpers when I have a wide range of hands, especially when I'm in position.

I love to call in these spots with hands that are not easily dominated. A player who limps in from middle or late position will very rarely have a premium pocket pair, so very few of my suited connectors (8-7, 7-6, etc.) and suited gappers (8-6, 7-5, etc.) will be completely dominated. And because my opponents are less likely to be holding premium cards, the hand is less likely to turn into the kind of big pot that I hate playing for with a small hand. (See "Big Hand Big Pot, Small Hand Small Pot," page 22.)

I believe that most of the value I get from calling a limper comes from my ability to exploit my superior position. The rest of the value comes from the chance that I'll be involved in a multiway pot—both of the blinds are likely to see the flop—and connect with the board in a big way. As a result I like to call limpers when I have hands that have a chance to stand up against three or four opponents—suited aces, suited connectors, and small or medium pocket pairs are all very good hands in this spot.

On the flip side, I find that hands like Q-J, Q-T, Q-9, Q-8, J-T, J-9, J-8, T-9, and T-8 can be very difficult to play in these kinds of pots. I have to remember that a player limped in front of me. What kind of hand are they likely to have? One that isn't strong enough to raise and isn't weak enough to fold. They are likely to hold cards like K-Q, K-J, K-T, Q-J, Q-T, or K-9. Flopping top pair with a low kicker* in these types of multiway pots can cost me a lot of money. If I flop a pair, I want to be the *only one* with that pair.

IN POSITION, SMOOTH-CALL A RAISER

One of the first times I played No Limit Hold'em, I was playing in a very small buy-in cash game. I had A-K suited under the gun, and I raised about three times the big blind. Everyone folded to the player on the button, who called. The blinds folded. I was ecstatic someone had called me with my powerhouse A-K.

The flop came J-8-5 rainbow. My stomach turned. It was immediately clear to me that playing No Limit Hold'em out of position was not a pleasant experience.

---

* Dave Foley, my cohost on *Celebrity Poker Showdown*, has coined the term "the Riverdancer" to describe a low kicker. It still cracks me up every time he says it. High kickers, in contrast, are "Rockettes."

Every good player in the world hates to be out of position at No Limit. The game is much more difficult for the player who is first to act after the flop.

When a player raises and everyone folds to me in late position, very often I've found it profitable to call with a wide range of hands. I want my opponent's stomach to turn. I want him to be uncomfortable.

When I make this play, I'm much more likely to call with 8-6 suited than I am to call with A-6. Calling with A-6 becomes unprofitable very quickly when I flop top pair–weak kicker against top pair–good kicker. But with 8-6 suited, it is very unlikely that my opponent will have one of those. Unless they have a pocket pair higher than 8s, I'm in very good shape. Three great things can happen for me in this situation:

♥ They can miss the flop completely, check to me, and I make a bet and take the pot.
♥ I'll make two pair or better on the flop about one out of thirty times.
♥ I can flop a good draw and get the right odds to continue.

I've found this play to be especially effective in the middle stages of a tournament when an average stack in middle or late position comes in for a raise and I call from the button. This play works wonders against players who espouse a very straightforward style after the flop: They check when they miss the flop and bet when they hit the pot.

PLAYING FROM THE SMALL BLIND

When everyone folds around to me and I'm in the small blind, there are several factors to consider:

♠ I am up against only one player.
♠ I am completely out of position on this round and every other round of betting.
♠ I already have half a bet committed to the pot.

Because I am out of position, I have accepted the fact that I will play at a negative expectation even against the most inexperienced and terrible players. My goal in the small blind, therefore, is to limit my losses.

The most important factor to consider is my opponent. Early in a tournament, if I get the opportunity, I will just complete the small blind to see what the big blind will do. Some players (including me) make an almost automatic raise when the small blind tries to see the flop cheaply. I want to know if I'm up against an opponent with that mind-set before the blinds increase and the antes kick in.

If my opponent is a very good player, I will often just fold. It is not going to be easy to extract money from him when I'm out of position.

——NO ANTES——

If there are no antes in play and the only money in the pot is the small blind and the big blind, I usually stick to a conservative game plan. I will play about 60–65% of the hands I'm dealt:

◆ Any ace
◆ Any pocket pair
◆ All suited kings, most unsuited kings
◆ Queens down to about Q-6*
◆ Jacks down to J-5*
◆ Most low suited connectors
◆ Most low suited one-gap connectors (6-4, 7-5)
◆ Some trashier hands

---

* With J-5 and Q-6, the five card gap is the largest gap that allows a two-way straight draw: J-5, flop 9-8-7; Q-6, flop T-9-8.

When I choose to play my hand, about 75% of the time I come in for a raise. My normal raise is about three to three-and-a-half times the big blind.

The other 25% of the time I choose to play my hand, I just complete the blind. When completing the bet, I try to make sure I'm doing so with a powerhouse hand about one time in every four. With that three to one ratio, if I am raised every time by the big blind, I will still come out ahead.

I assume that I'll get raised somewhere in the neighborhood of two times the big blind just about every time I complete the bet. The three times I am weak, I'll fold to the raise, losing a half blind each time. On the fourth time, however, I'll have a hand I can re-raise with and take the pot, winning an additional two big blinds.

Completing the Blind Breakdown

	25%	25%	25%	25%
My Hand	Weak	Weak	Weak	Strong
Action	Complete Fold	Complete Fold	Complete Fold	Complete Re-raise
Result	Lose 1/2	Lose 1/2	Lose 1/2	Win 2

Net = + 1/2

Once I reach the stage in a tournament when antes have come into play, if everyone folds to me, I will play about 95% of the hands I'm dealt in the small blind. I'll raise with about 75% of my hands, complete the bet with a weak hand about 15% of the time, complete the bet with a strong hand about 5% of the time, and throw the rest away.

Playing from the small blind is incredibly tough and requires a tremendous amount of experience. I just do my best to lose as little money as I can.

RAISING FROM THE BIG BLIND

On the rare occasions when everyone folds to the small blind, who just completes the bet, I will consider raising from the big blind with just about any two cards. Not only will the small blind have to play from out of position, but even if they call my raise, they will have to hit the flop hard enough to want to continue.

However, if the player in the small blind is tricky, I will very often just check hands like small pocket pairs in this spot. I don't want to raise, get re-raised, and have to fold.

I'll never show a bluff in this situation if it works—I want the player in the small blind to *always* put me on a good hand.

RAISE THE LIMPERS

Raising the limpers is one of my absolute favorite plays in No Limit Hold'em.

I see it all the time: An early position player limps in, the next player calls, the action gets around to me in late position.

I do my best to punish players who limp before the flop. When they are weak, I'm going to make them pay a price for playing weak hands in a weak way.

How good a hand is the early limper likely to have? How about the player or players who just called the limper? A raise here will often pick up the pot.

Courage is the key to this play. It doesn't take a good hand to win the pot, just situational awareness, a tight image, and the courage to fire the bullet.

I like to raise the size of the pot when I make this

play. If three players have limped in, there will be four-and-a-half big bets in the pot—the three limpers, plus the small and big blinds—so I'll raise about five or six times the size of the big blind.

If someone happens to call the raise, I will have a very good idea what kind of hand they are on. At worst I'm getting a great overlay on a hand that I get to play from position.

Many players will realize what I'm doing, but because I am in position, it will usually be a mistake for them to call or play back at me.

THE CHIP-SANDWICH PLAY

Let's say an early-position opponent, preferably a loose opponent, raises and gets called by one or more players. There is a lot of money in the pot. More important, the callers have very little chance of having a hand that will merit a call or a big re-raise—if they did, they would have raised themselves. Now it gets to me.

I "sandwich" the callers with a big raise.

If I raise and get the initial raiser to fold, the meat of the chips will very often be coming my way.

I am much more likely to make this play from the blinds than from the button. If I make this play from the button and one of the blinds happens to wake up with a great hand, it really doesn't matter what the initial raiser was betting with: My goose is cooked.

The sandwich raise becomes a fantastic play when I am down to about fifteen big blinds. Let's say I'm in the small blind. A loose player brings it in from early position for three times the big blind. Two players call. There are now ten-and-a-half blinds in the pot. I look down and find 8-7 suited. I raise all-in.

The initial raiser now has to make the tough decision as to whether to call a very significant raise. Even if my timing was off and he has a big hand—let's say A-K—and decides to call the bet, I'm still in pretty good shape. My 8-7 suited will beat his A-K about 41% of the time. I've invested fifteen big blinds and stand to win thirty-seven big blinds. I'm getting exactly the right odds on my money here.

I won't make this play with a hand that can easily be dominated, like an ace or king with a small kicker. I don't want to be 25% (or less) to win if I can help it. By making the all-in play, I completely negate my positional disadvantage. With all of my money in the pot, I can't be outplayed after the flop.

STEAL FROM THE CUTOFF

Swingers is one of my all-time favorite movies. There's a particularly great scene where Mike (Jon Favreau) gets advice from his friends on how long he should wait to call the beautiful baby he's just met:

MIKE: Tomorrow?

TRENT: No. . . .

SUE: Tomorrow, then a day.

TRENT: Yeah.

MIKE: So, two days?

TRENT: Yeah. I guess you could call it that.

SUE: Definitely. Two days. That's the industry standard. . . .

TRENT: I used to wait two days. Now everyone waits two days. Three days is kinda money now, don't you think?

SUE: Yeah. But two's enough not to look anxious. . . .

TRENT: Yeah, but three days is kinda money. . . .

It seems like the same thing is happening with "steal" raises before the flop. The steal from the button has become the industry standard. It's become so common that the blinds have started stealing back with their own re-raises.

I like to steal from the *cutoff** seat—even, dare I say it, from the seat just to the right of the cutoff—about twice as often as I do from the button. Sure, if my opponents are weak-tight, I'll still try the steal from the button. But then again, everyone steals from the button.

The cutoff is kinda money.

PREFLOP DOMINATION

A hand is said to be dominant over another hand when the hands share the high card but one kicker is better than another. It's the Rockette versus the Riverdancer. Avoiding domination *before the flop* is critical to success at No Limit Hold'em.

Take these examples:

A♣ K♦ vs. A♥ Q♠

---

* The *cutoff* is the seat immediately to the right of the dealer button.

The A-K completely dominates the A-Q, winning 74% of the time.

Contrast that match up to:

A♣ K♦ vs. 7♥ 2♠

The A-K beats the absolute worst hand in Hold'em only 67% of the time.

Or:

A♣ K♦ vs. Q♣ J♦

The A-K will win 65% of the time, just slightly worse than a two to one money favorite.

What these examples show me is that I want to get my money into the pot when I'm dominating my opponents, or at least when I'm not being dominated. It's the reason why many expert players rue hands like A-Q, A-J, and K-Q.

I would rather call the rest of my chips with 8-7 suited than I would with A-J. Think I'm crazy? Here's a computer simulation I ran:

Pit 8-7 suited against all combinations of A-A, K-K, A-K, A-Q, A-K suited, A-Q suited, and the 8-7 suited has nearly a 32% chance to win.

Now try A-J against the same hands. The A-J has only a 25.7% chance to win.

An interesting side note: Once I've pushed more than a third of my chips into the pot, the odds virtually force me to call off the rest of my money if I know—or at least strongly believe—that I'm not dominated.

PLAYING GREAT HANDS WHEN THEY RAISE

My opponent raises before the flop. I've got a very strong hand. Do I re-raise or just call?

Here are some of the factors I consider:

♣ Position

If I am in position, I am more likely to call. If I am out of position (playing from the blinds), I am very likely to re-raise and try to take the pot right away, negating my positional disadvantage.

♣ How good is my opponent?

If my opponent plays predictable poker after the flop, I am more likely to call. Against a better player, I am more apt to raise and attempt to take the pot before the flop.

After the flop there are dozens of hands my opponent can have and a dozen more hands he can represent. It is much easier to make decisions preflop against a tricky opponent.

♣ How strong is their hand?

If I think my opponent is on A-K or a big pair (K-K, Q-Q, J-J) and I have A-A, I will always re-raise. Many opponents can't wait to re-raise all-in with any of those hands. I can't wait to call them.

If my opponent does have K-K, Q-Q, or J-J and overcards hit the flop, I am very unlikely to get significant action postflop unless they flop the dreaded set.

♣ How do they like to play?

Against a loose-aggressive opponent who usually bets after the flop, I will often just smooth-call in position and try to trap him when he does.

If my opponent is apt to overcommit chips to the pot with only one pair, I will often just call and hope he catches exactly one pair to my overpair.

If I have A-K and my opponent is the type to take the third raise with J-J or a worse pair, I often just call before the flop. If I think he is the type of player to go broke with A-Q or A-J, obviously, I re-raise with A-K.

♣ How strong is my hand?

With K-K and Q-Q, I will almost always re-raise. An ace will hit the flop about 17% of the time when I have pocket kings, and an ace or a king will hit the flop about 35% of the times that I have pocket queens. This makes re-raising a much better play than calling with the hopes of trapping them on the flop.

♣ How many chips do I have?

If I have fewer chips than my opponent, I will re-raise more often than if I have more chips than my opponent. I want him to feel as though he can push me off my hand and not fear going broke.

When I choose to re-raise, I will usually re-raise about three or four times my opponent's bet—if he raises three times the size of the big blind, I'll make it nine times the big blind.

If I am re-raising from the blinds, I'll make it four times whatever my opponent bets. When I'm out of position, I want to take the pot down quickly.

ALL-IN BEFORE THE FLOP

Moving all-in before the flop is one of the most powerful plays in No Limit Hold'em. It's also one of the most dangerous. Under the following circumstances, however, I don't think it's ever wrong to push all-in:

- ♥ I have the best hand and I think my opponent will call.
- ♥ I have the worst hand and I think my opponent will fold and the pot is big enough to steal.
- ♥ I have the worst hand, but even if my opponent calls my all-in bet, I'll be getting the right pot odds.
- ♥ I may have the worst hand, but against an all-in bet, my opponent may fold. I have "folding equity" and equity from the chips in the pot.
- ♥ I will be getting the right pot odds no matter what my opponent holds.
- ♥ I have the best hand, my opponent has the right pot odds to call any bet I make, but an all-in bet might scare him into folding.

THE FOURTH RAISE
MEANS ACES

———————◆•◆———————

It was early in a tournament. The blinds were $100/$200. I had $24,000, a little bit more than the average stack at the time, and the table image of a tight-aggressive player.

Discovering pocket kings in early position, I made my standard raise to $600, three times the size of the big blind. Everyone folded to the small blind, a tight-aggressive professional, who re-raised to $1,400.

The action was back on me. Following my poker mantra—"With the best hand, raise!"—I did exactly that, upping the bet to $4,500. It took my opponent all of about fifteen seconds to move all-in.

I wish I could tell you that I laid down my kings, because, of course, he turned over American Airlines. Pocket aces. But I was too inexperienced at the time to recognize the situation for what it was:

The fourth raise means aces.

Now I know better. When I have a lot of chips in comparison to the blinds, I nearly always try to make the third raise with K-K so that I can get away from the hand if my opponent makes the fourth raise all-in. This requires a bit of planning on my part, as the following chart illustrates:

Stacks	Big Blind	My 1st Raise	Opp 2nd Raise	My 3rd Raise	Opp 4th Raise	Pot	To Call	Call All-In Odds	Correct Action
10,000	50	150	450	1,600	10,000	11,750	8,400	1.4-1	Fold
10,000	100	300	1,000	3,000	10,000	13,300	7,000	1.9-1	Fold
10,000	200	600	1,800	5,400	10,000	16,000	4,600	3.5-1	Fold
10,000	300	900	2,700	6,500	10,000	17,400	3,500	5.0-1	Call

I have to call if I'm getting better than 4.5-1 odds.

As a corollary, if I believe that my opponent is good enough to lay down their own kings, queens, or A-K to a fourth raise, I'll often just smooth-call the third raise when I have A-A. When the flop comes with three rags, I'll almost always bust him.

From my opponents' perspective, they've seen a tight player raise from early position. They re-raise. I re-reraise. How can they be sure that I don't have aces? The short answer is that they can't.

Of course, if I have a very loose image or if my opponent is loose or unreasonable, folding kings shouldn't be so automatic.

KNOW WHEN A PLAYER IS POT COMMITTED

———◆———

When a player enters a pot before the flop and has more than half of his chips in action, I consider him 100% pot committed. Given the opportunity, he'll put in the rest of his chips before the flop. If he doesn't get that chance, he'll likely use them all to chase the pot after the flop.

I will almost never try to bluff this player off his hand before the flop, and very rarely will I try to bluff after the flop. There's no point in bluffing if he's not going to fold.

Great tournament players can get away from their hand when they only have one third of their stack committed and they know they're beat. But no matter how good a player is, if he folds after committing more than two thirds of his stack, he is almost always making a mistake.

RE-RAISE TO ISOLATE

———◆———

I will often re-raise a short-stacked opponent in the hopes of isolating him in a heads-up showdown.

Consider this example: Everyone folds to me on the button, where I sit with A-J and a stack of forty big blinds. I raise three-and-a-half times the big blind. The small blind, with forty big blinds, calls, then the big blind moves all-in with his last seven big bets.

There are fourteen big bets in the pot, and it's going to cost me another three-and-a-half bets to call. I'm getting four to one on my money. (See "Pot Odds and Implied Odds," page 186.) Unless they've got pocket aces, I can't be any worse than a three to one underdog. Clearly, I've got to call the bet.

But consider what happens to the small blind if I decide to call. He's got to risk another three-and-a-half bets to win seventeen-and-a-half bets, the pot laying him odds of five to one. He's getting the right overlay to call with just about any two cards and could easily out-flop me.

My better play is to re-raise the big blind. The small blind didn't have a big enough hand to re-raise my initial raise, so it's pretty unlikely that he'll call. If I can get him to fold, I've managed to isolate the big blind and improve my chances of winning, and I'm still getting four to one odds from the pot.

An added benefit of this play is that even if the big blind wins the hand, he will not get the additional three-and-a-half bets that the small blind would have been virtually forced to call. Keeping an opponent as short stacked as possible is a very good idea.

The isolation re-raise is a great strategy to employ in a cash game or in the middle rounds of a tournament. It's not always the right play for the late stages of a tournament, however, as there may be a reason to keep the small blind in the hand. (See "Implicit Collusion Late in a Tournament," page 170.)

POCKET PAIRS IN MULTIWAY POTS

I remember a hand I played in a $5,000 No Limit Hold'em event at the 2002 *World Series of Poker*. It was still the first level of blinds ($25/$50) and no one had much more or less than the $5,000 in chips we'd started with. Three players limped into the pot. Seated in late position, I looked down to find 9-9.

I strongly suspected that I had the best hand and that a raise to about $300 could take down the pot. I decided, however, just to call. The small blind completed the bet, the big blind checked, and six players saw the flop:

A♠ J♠ 9♦

The blinds checked. Then all hell broke loose when the next player bet $300. The second player called. Another player raised to $1,500 before the action got to me! Of course, having flopped a set of nines, I moved all-in, and I got called by what turned out to be A♦ J♦. I was 78.7% to win and my hand held up. I raked in a $12,000 pot.

Had I raised before the flop, I would have won a paltry $225, barely a ripple to my $5,000 stack. By merely calling I traded my small preflop positive expectation for huge implied odds and, thanks to a little good fortune, became the new chip leader at the table and tournament.

When the blinds and antes are small in comparison to my stack size, I try to play my small pocket pairs (two to six) and middle pocket pairs (seven to jack) as cheaply as possible and against as many opponents as possible. I want to flop a set and have the best chance possible that an opponent will make a good (but second-best) hand. With these pairs I'll either win a very big pot or lose a very small pot.

AFTER THE FLOP

As multi-tournament champion T. J. Cloutier says of No Limit Hold'em, "If I don't flop to it, I'm done with it." For the most part I'm inclined to agree.

Once the flop arrives, I've seen five of the seven cards I'll have to make my hand. There are only two cards left to come—which presents me with a pretty clear picture of what my final hand is going to look like—and basically just two decisions to be made:

♠ Should I put chips into the pot?
♠ If so, how many?

There are a lot of factors to consider when making these decisions, but the most important, even more important than my actual hand, is this:

♠ What are my opponents likely to hold?

Once I have put my opponents on a hand, all I have to do is force them to make a mistake, such as:

♠ Folding a better hand than I have
♠ Calling a big bet with a worse hand than I have
♠ Failing to bet or raise when I have the worst hand or a draw

Almost every decision I make after the flop is intended to help my opponent make one of these mistakes.

FIRST TO THE POT WINS

When the board is paired, the chance of someone having actually "caught a piece" of the flop is much smaller than if there are cards of three different ranks on the board. I've found that the first player to bet at a paired board will very often win the pot.

I will frequently lead out and bet no matter what my hand is when the flop comes something like:

6-6-4
9-9-2
T-3-3
K-6-6
K-K-6

This play is particularly effective when I am in the blinds and against limpers. Being in the blinds seems to make it more credible that I have a hand that flopped trips.

When I lead into a paired board, I like to bet about one third to one half of the pot. I find that when I bet more or less than that amount, my opponents tend to read it as weakness and will often try to raise me off my hand.

I generally bet these flops with exactly the same-size bet when I "hit" the flop. By betting when I've "got it" and betting when I don't, I make it very difficult for my opponents to play optimally against me.

I am slightly more conservative with my bluff attempts and more aggressive with my bets when the board has two cards of the same suit.

HEADS-UP POSTFLOP

Multiway action in No Limit Hold'em can get extremely complicated. I prefer simple. When I'm seated at a full table, I am usually aiming to get heads-up with a single opponent before the flop.

Heads-up poker is much easier to play. Since I am almost always raising the pot if I'm the first person in, I can use the following criteria to analyze each head-to-head confrontation:

♦ My preflop raise—backed by my image as a tight-aggressive player—should lead my opponent to believe that I have a good hand regardless of its actual strength. (If I don't have a tight-aggressive image, well, I have to take that into account.)

♦ A player with unpaired hole cards will hit a pair or better on the flop only about one out of three times.

♦ A player with paired hole cards will hit a set or better on the flop about one out of eight times.

There are only six possible ways for a heads-up hand to play out.

1. I am the first person to enter the pot before the flop and make my standard raise. A player with better position than I have calls, both blinds fold.

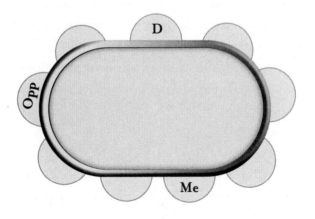

Since I raised before the flop, it's usually in my best interest to make a show of strength after the flop. I will make what is called a "continuation bet" about 65% of the time.

I will make this bet—about half the size of the pot—the 35% of the time that I flop a pair or better and the 10–15% of the time that I flop some kind of draw. Add those up and you'll see that in about 15–20% of all cases, I am making a continuation bet having missed the flop entirely.

Remember that my opponent is only going to flop a hand about 35% of the time, and unless they've flopped some kind of super draw, they probably aren't getting the right pot odds (three to one) to chase a draw.

If I can risk half the pot to win a full pot 65% of the time, I should show a net profit of one-and-a-half full pots every ten times I make the play. I will have invested ten half-pot bets, or five full pots, but I should win six-and-a-half full pots along the way.

2. I raise before the flop and get called by a player who has worse position than I have.

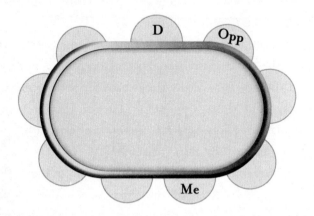

I do not like to slowplay. If my opponent checks to me—a sign that they've missed the flop—I'm going to bet about 85% of the time. I'll play a little more carefully against a player who loves to check-raise, maybe betting 65% of the time they check.

3. Another player raises before the flop. I call from better position.

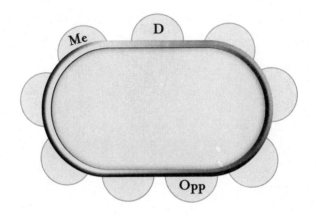

If my opponent checks to me, they've either missed the flop or they are trying to trap me. I will bet about 50% of the time.

If I flop a two-way straight draw—especially against a player who loves to check-raise—I will rarely bet. I'll take the free chance to catch my card on the turn. With a more difficult-to-fill gut-shot straight draw, I am more likely to try to take the pot with a bet on the flop. Same goes for a flush draw—I will usually bet this hand as it will be very difficult to get paid off in a big way should I make the flush on the turn.

4. Another player raises before the flop. I call from worse position.

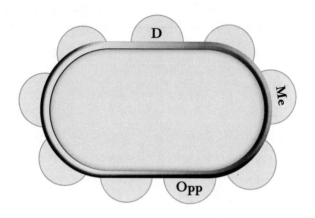

This scenario hardly merits consideration because it happens so rarely. I hate, hate, hate playing No Limit Hold'em out of position. When I call out of position, I am usually doing so with hands that will hit the flop hard (a small to medium pocket pair, suited connectors) or will be easy to fold after the flop. When I hit my hand, I'll usually bet right out and hope to get raised.

5. The small blind limps in. I check from the big blind.
   I am in superior position. If they check to me on the flop, I'm going to bet about 75–80% of the time. If they bet, I'll very often raise even without a great hand.

6. A player limps in before the flop. The small blind folds; I check from the big blind.

I'm going to bet about 65% of the time after the flop, on similar reasoning to scenario three above. I'll bet slightly more often because my opponent is very likely weak and it will be harder for them to call. I will check-raise about 10–15% of the time, and I don't always have to have a hand to do it, though I will have a hand about 75% of the time I check-raise here. I am more likely to bet if the flop has high or low cards, less likely to bet if it is full of jacks, tens, or nines. I expect my opponent to be playing middle cards when he limps.

AGAINST MULTIPLE OPPONENTS

Everything becomes more difficult when I'm facing more than one opponent after the flop. Bluffing works less frequently, as there are more players to bluff out. There is also a much bigger likelihood that I'm up against a great hand. Pots contested by multiple players before the flop are very often contested after the flop. The pots are bigger and there are many more dangers.

Here are some general guidelines that I use against multiple opponents:

♣ I very rarely make a stone-cold bluff after the flop. Even if everyone checks to me, if I miss the flop, I just let it go. The more players in the pot, the less likely I am to try to bluff.

♣ If I think I have the best hand, I nearly always bet. I almost never slowplay in a multiway pot. I bet and hope that someone can raise.

♣ My bets in multiway pots are designed to narrow the field even if I don't win the pot right away. I don't mind winning the pot right away when I'm up against multiple opponents.

♣ Check-raising in a multiway pot is an overused tactic that can easily backfire. I am much more inclined to bet than check-raise.

♣ If any of my middle-action opponents are short stacked, I am more likely to go for a check-raise. Consider this example: I have 6-6 in the big blind and I get a free look at the flop after two opponents in middle position limp into the pot. I'm first to bet after the flop. The flop comes K♦ Q♥ 6♦. The player immediately to my left has a short stack. If I bet right out and my short-stacked opponent has a good hand, he'll call. But then the last player to act may get good enough odds to call as well—I won't have a chance to put significant pressure on my third opponent. If I check, my short-stacked opponent will bet all-in and it will put the last player to act in a tough spot. Very often, that opponent will call and try to break the short stack. This is a great opportunity to check-raise and isolate with a ton of dead money in the pot.

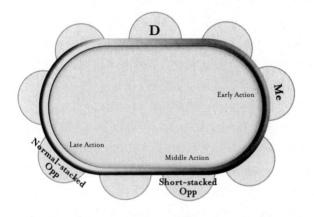

♣ If the late-action opponents are short stacked, I almost never check-raise or check-call. I don't want to get trapped by the middle-position player. When the short stack is in the late-action position, I'll go ahead and bet right out if I'm going to commit chips to the pot.

BETTING TO SLOW DOWN
AN OPPONENT

Let's say I flop a good draw to a straight or a flush. Now I check to my opponent, who makes a bet the size of the pot. I am getting two to one odds on my money should I call, but the odds are four to one against my completing my draw on the turn. I have to fold my hand. They priced me out with a nice bet.

Sometimes when I flop a good draw, I will lead at the pot with a small bet in the hopes of slowing down my opponent. This play is best made against:

♥ Players who are hesitant to raise
♥ Players who are prone to slowplay a made hand
♥ Aggressive players who will bet big if I check to them

Let's say I lead out with a bet one fourth the size of the pot and my opponent just calls. I am getting five to one odds from the pot to make my bet on the turn. In other words I'm not only getting good value for my bet, but I've allowed my opponent to make a mistake by not betting enough against me.

If my opponent picks up on this tendency and starts raising my small bets, I will sometimes bet a very strong hand in the same way.

DOUBLE GUT-SHOT STRAIGHT DRAWS

I would rather have a double gut-shot straight draw (DGSD) than an open-ended straight draw (OESD). The double-gutter is much more difficult for my opponent to read.

For example, when the board looks like this:

$$Q\spadesuit\ 9\spadesuit\ 4\clubsuit$$

most opponents will be very wary of putting a lot of chips into the pot if a king or an eight comes on the turn. They are scared (and rightly so) that I had an OESD with a J-T in the hole.

But say the board looks like this:

$$J\clubsuit\ 8\spadesuit\ 5\spadesuit$$

and I have 9-7 in the hole. Thanks to my DGSD, I still have eight outs—any ten or six will complete my straight—but my opponent probably won't be as afraid to continue with their hand. A six on the turn in this example looks far less intimidating than the eight in the previous one.

One small problem with the DGSD is that one of my outs might make a higher straight for an opponent. Take the example above. A ten on the turn will make my straight, but it will also give anyone holding a Q-9 a more powerful straight than mine. I will have to proceed with a little more caution.

HANDS TO BRING TO WAR

I don't always need to make a hand on the flop to "go to war"—a very good draw is often enough, especially against a player who I believe has only one pair. In almost all of the cases below, I will make the best hand more than 50% of the time and can therefore play very aggressively after the flop:

My Opponent	My Hand	The Board	My Chances

A straight flush draw:

My Opponent	My Hand	The Board	My Chances
A♠ K♦	J♥ T♥	A♣ 9♥ 8♥	56.3%

A flush draw and an overcard to the board:

My Opponent	My Hand	The Board	My Chances
K♠ Q♦	A♥ T♥	K♣ 9♥ 8♥	47.2%

Two overcards to the board, straight
and backdoor flush draw:

My Opponent	My Hand	The Board	My Chances
8♠ 8♦	K♥ Q♥	J♣ T♦ 2♥	55.3%

Flush draw with one pair
(a pair different from my opponent's):

My Opponent	My Hand	The Board	My Chances
A♠ K♠	Q♥ 7♥	K♥ Q♣ 3♥	50.1%

Moving all-in or even calling all-in with these draws against one pair is almost never "wrong." As usual, however, it's best to be the aggressor. By betting first I have two ways to win: My opponent might fold *or* I can draw and make a winner.

By playing very aggressively with my big draws, I am able to get my opponent to put in a lot of chips when I have a great, made hand. They have to guess if I have a draw or the nuts. In the first case I've got a good shot of making a winner. In the second case they are drawing very slim.

BOARD TEXTURE

When I'm thinking about my actions after the flop or turn, I look to the "texture" of the board—what cards are in play, and how they might have interacted with my opponent's likely starting hands—to help determine if and how much I will bet.

My normal betting range is one third of the pot to the full size of the pot. The texture of the board dictates where in that range I choose to bet.

♠ How strong is my hand with respect to all likely hands for my opponent?

If I have a very strong hand with respect to all likely starting hands for my opponent, I'll usually go for the lower end of the spectrum, betting around a third of the pot. I want my opponent to call.

If I have a moderate-strength hand with respect to all likely starting hands for my opponent, I'll likely bet two thirds of the pot. I want my opponents to fold some hands that are better than my hand and call with some hands that are worse than my hand.

If I have a weak hand with respect to all likely starting hands for my opponent and I want to bet, I'll bet the pot. I want my opponents to fold hands that are better than my hand.

♠ How likely is my hand to improve?

If my hand is unlikely to improve, I tend to bet more than two thirds of the pot. I want to take this pot now.

If my hand is somewhat likely to improve, say about 15–20% of the time, I am more apt to bet two thirds of the pot.

If my hand is very likely to improve, about 34% or more of the time, I am more apt to bet half of the pot.

♠ How likely is my opponent to have "hit the flop" and have a pair or better?

If my opponent is very unlikely to have hit the flop and have top pair or better, I tend to bet a third of the pot whether I think I have the best hand or not.

If my opponent is likely to have flopped exactly one pair, and I think I have the best hand, I tend to bet two thirds of the pot.

If my opponent is likely to have flopped two pair or better and I think I have the best hand, I tend to bet the size of the pot. If I don't think I have the best hand, I'll almost never bet.

♠ How likely is my opponent to have a primary draw (eight or more outs)?

If I think my opponent is likely to have a primary draw and I think I have the best hand, I'm likely to bet the size of the pot.

If I think my opponent has a primary draw and there is a good chance I don't have the best hand, I'll almost never bet.

When the four factors above lead to different conclusions about how much to bet, I average the recommendations and bet that amount. Over time the amount to bet based on the texture of the board becomes almost automatic.

BET GOOD HANDS

After the flop I almost always bet my good hands. My opponents will often raise me because they fear my image, because they want to find out where I'm at, and because they don't want to give me a cheap draw. There is no point in check-raising when I can re-raise an opponent who has raised me.

This is especially important if I think my opponent has top pair or an overpair and I've flopped a set. Let's say my opponent has raised before the flop with a big pocket pair: A-A, K-K, or Q-Q. I've called with a small pocket pair, say sixes, and flopped trips when the board comes 9-6-2. If I lead at the pot with about a half-pot bet, my opponent will generally try to get all the money in. I'll oblige. He'll be drawing very slim.

AFTER FLOPPING TWO PAIR

Flopping two pair is worthy of celebration, or at the very least a bet or a raise. I am almost always committed to seeing the turn card. In fact, I can't remember a time when I folded two pair after the flop against a single opponent unless the board had three cards of the same suit.

Not all two pair are created equal. There are three different varieties—top two pair, top and bottom pair, and bottom two pair—and each has its own unique properties and strategic implications. One constant among all three, however, is how unlikely I am to improve my hand. I will only draw to a full house or better 17% of the time. In other words I've got to plan on winning with two pair.

——TOP TWO PAIR——

When I flop top two pair, I want to get as much money into the pot as possible. I'm almost certain to have the best hand, as there's only a small chance my opponent has flopped bottom set, and an even smaller chance (given my two cards) that they've flopped top or middle set.

In a perfect world, my opponent has flopped top pair with little or no chance of drawing to a straight or a flush. I am in line to win a big pot with very little chance of losing.

Here are some scenarios and my chances of winning:

Me	My Opponent	The Flop	My Chances
A♣ T♦	A♥ Q♦	A♥ T♣ 4♥	85%
J♣ T♦	K♦ Q♥	J♥ T♠ 3♣	68%
J♣ T♦	A♦ A♣	J♥ T♠ 3♣	73%
J♣ T♦	4♠ 4♣	J♥ T♠ 4♦	17%

When I flop top two pair with two cards that are close together in rank, I will bet and raise aggressively as there will likely be straight possibilities.

If my opponent plays back at me, raising or re-raising, it's often difficult to know if he's flopped a set or merely lost his mind. Against a bad player who will overcommit his chips with top pair or an overpair, I can almost never throw this hand away. Against a good player, however, I will remain wary and attentive. Good players do not commit their entire stack to the hand with only one pair. If a good player is firing back at me with both barrels, it is possible, albeit rare, to get away from my hand.

——BOTTOM TWO PAIR——

I play with similar aggression when I've flopped bottom two pair. An opponent who has flopped top pair has only five outs to improve their hand. My hand will still be the best hand about 88% of the time after the turn card, and about 76% of the time after the river card. For example:

Me	My Opponent	The Flop	My Chances
6♣ 5♦	A♦ Q♥	A♥ 6♦ 5♠	76%

In this scenario only the two aces and three queens in the deck help my opponent to improve their hand.

If the board pairs on the turn and river (A-6-5-8-8 in the example above, for instance), I'll be counterfeited and my two pair will become dog meat. I play bottom two pair after the turn card very aggressively and look to take the pot right away.

——TOP AND BOTTOM PAIR——

While it may seem counterintuitive, I am most vulnerable when I flop top and bottom pair. Why is this hand more vulnerable than flopping bottom two pair? Because an opponent with top pair or an overpair has an extra out.

Me	My Opponent	The Flop	My Chances
A♣ 5♦	A♦ Q♥	A♥ 9♣ 5♠	73%
K♣ 8♣	A♦ A♣	K♦ T♥ 8♠	73%

My opponent has six outs. Looking at the first example, not only do I have to dodge a queen, but if the nine arrives, my two pair become the same as theirs, aces and nines. Only they've got a queen kicker to my five, and I'm looking at a trip to the bathroom to throw up.

AFTER FLOPPING A SET

When I flop a set, I try to remember that my goal is to get my opponent to make the biggest mistake possible. Any money they put into the pot is likely to be dead money.

Here is how I normally go about it:

——OUT OF POSITION——

If I'm first to act (under the gun, out of position, or with players checking in front of me but one or more players left to act), I will look at the board and determine if my opponent is likely to have flopped the top pair or an overpair. If yes, I will almost always bet. I bet because I want to get raised.

If I do not think that my opponent has flopped top pair or an overpair, I will check (slowplay), hoping to induce a bluff or hoping that they'll check and improve a little on the turn.

Here's an example of a hand I played in a *WPT* event during the inaugural season. A tight player raised it three times the big blind from middle/late position. I put him on a big ace or a big pair and decided to call from the big blind with pocket fives, or in the parlance of the Tiltboys,

"Presto!" The flop came K-8-5. I bet the pot. Now, if he had A-K or K-Q, I would have had him in a very tough situation. If he had A-A, I would have had him in a nearly impossible situation. With any of those hands, he almost certainly had to raise, which is exactly what I wanted to happen. It is very unlikely that a check-raise here would have allowed me to extract any additional money. He moved all-in with A-K, and I beat him to the middle.

A few rounds later I was in the small blind with 8-8. Another late-position, medium-tight player raised it three times the big blind. I put him on A-K, A-Q, or A-J and decided to call. The flop was T-8-2. (Yes, I flop a lot of sets!) I checked, hoping that this player would take a stab at the pot. I wasn't too worried about giving him a free card, as he was likely to bet most of the hands that could improve with a free card right there on the flop. Whatever risk might have been involved was mitigated by the excellent chance that he'd feel compelled to bluff at the pot with any A-K, A-Q, or A-J. Most players are unlikely to call or raise a bet having missed the flop with one of those hands, but many of the same players are more than happy to bet at the pot if they're allowed the chance to fire first. My opponent made a huge bluff wih A-K, and I busted him.

——IN POSITION——

If my opponent checks to me, I have to decide if they are genuinely weak or if they are going for a check-raise.

If I think they have a weak hand, I'll almost always check and hope that they catch up a little on the turn card.

If I think they have a good hand and they are going for a check-raise, I'll make a pot-size bet and pray they come over the top with a big check-raise.

If the flop has straight or flush possibilities, I will almost always bet, usually about three quarters of the pot.

If my opponent bets into me, I have a couple of plays available to me. I can call and hope to trap them for bigger money on the turn, or simply raise right away.

Against players who overplay top pair, I will almost always raise.

If the board is queen-high or lower, I'll almost always raise and hope that my opponent re-raises. Why? If an ace or king comes on the turn (something that will happen about one time in seven) and my opponent doesn't have one, they're likely to shut down, killing any further action. I really want my opponent to have top pair or two pair after the turn card.

If the board looks headed toward a straight or a flush, I will generally raise and make them pay to chase me.

If the board contains an ace and my opponent bets, I'll always raise. Most opponents are not willing to lay down top pair after the flop.

——SET OVER SET——

When I flop a set, I never worry about my opponent having a bigger set. If both players start with a pocket pair, set over set will happen after the flop only about one out of one hundred times. Against those odds, I'm willing to risk going broke.

AFTER FLOPPING TRIPS

When the board is paired and I've flopped trips, it is a cause to celebrate. There are two ways to flop trips:

High Trips	
My Hand: 9-7	The Board: 9-9-3
My Hand: A-Q	The Board: A-A-4

Low Trips	
My Hand: 9-7	The Board: A-9-9
My Hand: A-Q	The Board: K-Q-Q

Here are some of the considerations I take into account when deciding how to proceed:

♦ If I've flopped high trips and I put my opponent on an overpair to the board, I will nearly always bet or raise. I want my opponent to re-raise.

Me: J-T	My Opponent: A-A or K-K	The Board: J-J-4

♦ If I've flopped low trips and I put my opponent on an overpair to the board or paired with the high card on the board, I nearly always bet or raise. I want my opponent to re-raise.

Me: 9-7	My Opponent: A-A or K-K	The Board: J-9-9
Me: 9-7	My Opponent: A-K or A-Q	The Board: A-7-7

♦ If I believe it is likely that my opponent has a straight draw or a flush draw, I am very likely to bet.

♦ If I have flopped high trips and I believe it is likely that my opponent flopped a middle pair, I'll often slow-play or go for a check-raise.

| Me: A-5 | My Opponent: 8-8, 9-9, or T-T | The Board: A-A-2 |
| Me: A-5 | My Opponent: K-Q or Q-J | The Board: A-A-Q |

♦ If I flopped low trips and I believe it is likely that my opponent flopped a middle pair, I'll often slowplay or go for a check-raise.

| Me: K-5 | My Opponent: 8-8, 9-9, or T-T | The Board: A-5-5 |

♦ If I have an ace with a low kicker and I flop high trips, I will always bet if my opponent checks to me. I want to get raised if they have me beat so I can figure out where I stand (though it will be very difficult to get away from the hand and fold). I will go for a check-raise if I'm out of position. When I check-raise, if they then re-raise me, I can be fairly certain that I'm beat. The key in this situation is to make my opponent tell me as quickly as possible if they have me beat. This is a good pot to understand that I will either win a very small pot when I'm ahead or lose a very big pot when I'm beat.

| Me: A-2 | My Opponent: ?-? | The Board: A-A-3 |

♦ If I've flopped trips with the best kicker possible, all the money is going into the pot if given the opportunity. I don't usually worry about my opponent having flopped a full house. I find that it is much more likely that they've flopped trips as well.

| Me: A-K | My Opponent: A-Q | The Board: A-A-5 |
| Me: A-8 | My Opponent: ?-? | The Board: Q-8-8 |

In general, if my opponent expects me to slowplay trips, I will usually bet or raise. I want to confuse them. If my opponent expects me to bet or raise with my trips, I will usually slowplay.

AFTER FLOPPING A STRAIGHT

There are several different ways to flop a straight. I can have the "smart end"—the highest possible straight—or the "dumb" or "ignorant" end, which leaves me vulnerable to a higher straight. The cards on the board may have zero, one, or two gaps between them. Each type of straight requires a slightly different strategy after the flop. The most important underlying fact, however, is that the hand I've flopped is most likely the hand I'm going to finish with.* It's probably not going to improve, and can only get worse.

——THE SMART END, ZERO, —— OR ONE GAP

When I flop the smart end with zero or one gap on the board, I flop the nut straight (the best straight possible), a very powerful hand.

Me	The Flop
K-Q	J-T-9
Q-10	J-9-8

I'll usually bet about half the pot if the flop is unsuited, two thirds of the pot if the flop has two of the same suit, or the full size of the pot if all three cards are of the same suit. I'm hoping to get action, and I've found that betting here nets me more action than

---

* Unless I have a flush draw or a runner-runner flush draw. With a flush draw, my hand will improve to a flush about 35% of the time; with a runner-runner flush draw, I'll make a flush about 6.4% of the time.

slowplaying. If I fail to bet the flop, there are as many as fourteen scare cards that can cause an opponent to shut down on the turn. For example, in the first case above, any king, queen, eight, or seven is likely to make an opponent with top pair or a set think twice about putting any more money into the middle. I might as well bet the flop and get as much as I can before a scare card hits.

——THE DUMB END, ZERO,—— OR ONE GAP

When I flop the dumb end of the straight with zero or one gap on the board, I play hyperaggressively and try to protect my hand.

Me	The Flop
8-7	J-T-9
T-7	J-9-8

There aren't too many cards that can come on the turn that will make me happy. In the first example above, I'm going to be very scared if a king, a queen, or an eight arrives. Any 7 will cause my opponent to shut down.

In this case I'm almost always going to bet the pot. In fact, this is one case where I will often overbet the pot and try to take it down right away.

I am very wary of playing 9-8, suited or otherwise. If the flop comes Q-J-T and I'm up against A-K, I am going to lose a lot of money. An awful lot of money. A computer analysis shows that 9-8 played against the sorts of hands that an opponent is willing to risk a lot of money on—A-K, K-K, Q-Q, J-J, T-T, K-Q, K-J, Q-J, K-T, K-9—my pot equity is just 48.5% with that flop.*

——TWO-GAP STRAIGHTS——

There are two ways to flop a two-gap straight and both play just about the same.

Me	The Flop
J-T	Q-9-8
J-9	Q-T-8

In this scenario there are only six cards that can come on the turn that will slow my opponent down: any

---

* For adventurous souls who would like to experiment with computer analysis, the best tool I've been able to find on the Internet is called the "Poker Stove" and can be found at www.pokerstove.com.

three of my highest rank and any three of my lowest rank. That's going to happen about six out of forty-seven times, or about 13% of the time.

If the board is suited, I usually bet about two thirds of the pot. Otherwise, I bet about half the pot.

❖ SLEAZY BAR TRICK ❖

Pick the sucker, take out a deck of cards, and say, "I'm going to remove eight cards from this deck, and I bet you can't make a five-card straight." If they take the bet, remove the tens and fives, hand them the deck, order a double, and then toast me and the *Little Green Book*. All straights contain either a five or a ten.

AFTER FLOPPING A FLUSH

With two suited cards I will flop a flush about 0.84% of the time, or about 1 out of every 119 times I play them. The real problem with flopping a flush, of course, is that my opponents are very unlikely to give me any real action.

When I flop the nut flush (the best flush possible), I will very often resort to slowplaying. I've been known to slowplay all the way to the river if no one wants to bet after the flop or after the turn. The problem with this approach, however, is that another flush card on the turn or the river—something that will happen about 17% of the time—will *really* kill the action unless my opponent manages to simultaneously make a flush *and* lose his mind.

On those rare occasions that I do flop a flush, I generally do the following:

♣ Silently thank the stars above—I just flopped a flush!
♣ If I think there's a good chance that my opponent has top pair or an overpair to the board, I'll make a bet about the size of the pot. Most opponents won't give me credit for the flush, expecting me to slowplay it, and will often be confused by my bet.
♣ If I don't think my opponent flopped top pair or an overpair, I'll often check or make a weak-looking bet, maybe a third of the pot, hoping he catches a piece (or, better yet, decides to bluff) on the turn.
♣ If I don't have the nut flush, I'm going to bet about half of the pot and hope that my opponent

calls with the nut flush draw. He will be making a big mistake, as only seven cards (14%) will help him on the turn. He's getting three to one odds from the pot, but odds are six to one against him making his hand.

If he gets cute and raises me with the nut flush draw, I will almost always re-raise. If he's already flopped a higher flush, I'm probably going broke.

AFTER FLOPPING A FULL HOUSE

When I am fortunate enough to flop a full house or better, it is a great feeling, of course, but very often short-lived. It is very difficult to get action after flopping a full house, and very often I win only a small pot.

There are four ways to flop a full house, and I play each in a slightly different way:

My Hand	The Board
A-5	A-A-5

When I flop a full house like this, I will usually just go ahead and bet out or raise if my opponent bets into me. I really want my opponent to have the ace here and get frisky. It is very possible that all the money will be going into the pot after a flop like this if they have an ace. It is equally likely that no money will be going into the pot if they don't have an ace. I will bet about half the pot in most circumstances. At best, my opponent will be drawing to three outs. (Incidentally, I will often bet this flop even if I don't have an ace.)

My Hand	The Board
A-5	A-5-5

Again, this is a good flop to just go ahead and bet. If my opponent has an ace, I'll get action. If they don't have an ace, slowplaying will be ineffective. The big danger in slowplaying comes when I'm up against a pocket pair. In this case, if my opponent has, say, T-T, they have a 4% chance to catch a ten on the turn and break me.

My Hand	The Board
A-A	A-5-5

This is the only instance when I slowplay a full house on the flop. In this case it is very unlikely that my opponent will be able to catch up, but if they do, they'll be toast.

I will not slowplay, however, if I put my opponent on an overpair to the board. For instance, if I have T-T and the flop comes T-8-8 and I put my opponent on a big pocket pair, I'll just go ahead and bet, and I'll bet about the size of the pot. I want to make them put a lot of money into the pot before the turn card can potentially kill my action. For instance, suppose I believe my opponent is likely on K-K or Q-Q. If I check/call and an ace comes on the turn, my opponent will very likely get scared off and it will be more difficult to get them to commit a big mistake.

My Hand	The Board
5-5	A-A-5

This hand is more vulnerable than it looks and I play it aggressively. Against an opponent with any ace (but not A-5), this hand is only going to stand up about 77% of the time. For this reason I will play it very aggressively and bet and raise and re-raise if given the opportunity.

Here are some other things I think about:

♥ If the board is suited or "straightening," I am more likely to bet and hope that my opponent has the flush or straight draw—they will probably call my bet, but they'll be drawing dead. If the flush card comes on the turn, I'll go ahead and bet out and hope to get raised or check-raised.

♥ Many opponents expect to be slowplayed. When I go ahead and bet my good hand, they often think they are in better shape than when I slowplay. The slowplay is such a strong play that it will tip them off as to the true strength of my hand. When I go ahead and bet, I'll usually get more action.

♥ Against players prone to overbetting the pot on bluffs, I am more apt to go for a slowplay.

AFTER FLOPPING FOUR OF A KIND

It doesn't happen very often, but when it does, I try not to smile and then I slowplay, slowplay, slowplay.

My best friend, Rafe Furst, was playing in a tournament at the Commerce Casino in Los Angeles in 2005, where he found himself seated next to "Spider-Man" Tobey Maguire. Tobey limped in from middle position, leading Rafe to raise from the button with A-7 suited. Tobey called.

The flop came A-2-2. Tobey checked to Rafe, who bet half the pot. Tobey called. The turn was a seven, the perfect card for Rafe to hang himself, which is exactly what he did after Tobey checked for a second time. Rafe bet about $3,000—the size of the pot—leaving him with only $500 or so. Tobey correctly decided that he had Rafe pot committed and moved all-in.

Rafe called. Tobey turned over pocket deuces and raked in the pot with a little smile that all the acting talent in the world couldn't have prevented.

AFTER FLOPPING A DRAW

Drawing hands are overrated in No Limit Hold'em when playing against expert competition. By betting correctly, experts usually make it prohibitively expensive to go for a draw.

There are two primary drawing situations: a two-way straight draw (either open-ended or double gut-shot) and a flush draw.

When I flop a primary draw, here are some of the factors I consider when deciding to bet or check:

- ♠ If I was the first player to enter the pot, I entered the pot for a raise before the flop. I almost always bet or raise in these situations because I want to follow through with my preflop bet and "keep the lead" in the hand. I want my opponent to guess.

- ♠ If my hand has outs other than a flush, I play very aggressively. (See "Hands to Bring to War," page 70.) For example, if I have A♦ 5♦ and the flop comes 8♦ 6♦ 4♥, I'll play hyperaggressively. A seven will make a straight, and an ace may give me the best hand as well.

- ♠ If I am out of position, I am more likely to check/call if my opponent habitually underbets the pot.

- ♠ If I am in position, I am more likely to check and take a free look at the turn card if my opponent habitually check-raises.

- ♠ If I sense weakness or uncertainty, I'll almost always bet.

- ♠ If I have the nut flush draw, I am more likely to slow-play than if I have a non—nut flush draw. Very often if

I make a flush on the turn, my opponent will have outs in the form of a higher flush.

♠ If I am pot committed, I try to be the player making the last move. I want to raise or bet all-in, not call all-in, if possible. I gain "folding equity" when I make the last move.

♠ When I have a straight draw and the board has two or three cards of the same suit, I am more likely to bet/raise than I am when the board is three-suited.

♠ If my opponent is short stacked, I'm very likely to go ahead and bet.

♠ If the board is paired, I'm more likely to bet my draw. This is because it is more difficult for my opponent to have a hand worthy of continuing, and they'll be afraid that I've flopped three of a kind, which will make it less likely that they'll be able to raise me. When I bet in these situations, a bet of about a third of the pot usually gets the job done.

♠ The implied odds of a flush draw are almost always lower than the implied odds of a straight draw. Many opponents will simply shut right down if the flush card comes on the turn.

Playing draws successfully is a big part of playing No Limit Hold'em well.

WHEN I BET AND A GOOD
PLAYER CALLS

I have a good hand. I raise before the flop. A good player calls me, and I'm out of position. After the flop, I bet the pot, giving any draw insufficient odds to call. A good player calls me anyway.

This is one of the scariest situations in No Limit Hold'em. Good players very rarely call. Good players raise or fold. Good players who call a bet after the flop are very, very often slowplaying a monster hand.

AFTER THE TURN

After the turn card hits, I've seen six of the seven cards available to make a hand. Draws have become nearly meaningless in the face of any significant action, as with only one card to come, I'll complete a straight or a flush less than 20% of the time.

The turn will very often do what its name suggests: turn the tide of the hand. An opponent who took the worst of it with a call on the flop might catch up. Or, more likely, the drawer missed the draw and the leader is still the leader.

Aggression after the turn is still critical to success.

I almost never give a free river card to my opponent if I think I have the best hand. In general, I'm going to bet a reasonable amount relative to the pot, which by this point will normally be quite large. Taking it down and adding those chips to my stack is vital.

That means that if I'm first to act with what I think is the best hand, I'm not going to get cute with a check-raise. I'm betting. If my opponent checks to me, I'm going to bet my hand if I think I have the best of it.

The turn card is not the time to get tricky. Successful No Limit Hold'em players who have the best hand on the turn do not want to see the river unless their opponent is drawing very slim or paying a very dear price to see the last card.

WHEN I IMPROVE MY HAND

If the turn card helped my hand, I will usually bet or raise when given the opportunity. Here are some of the factors I consider:

♥ If I played passively after the flop (that is, I checked or just called) and I've improved my hand, I'm likely to play very aggressively after improving my hand.

♥ If I played aggressively after the flop, I am more likely to play the hand slower after improving my hand significantly.

♥ In nearly all cases, if my opponent bets into me and I've improved my hand, I will raise.

♥ In nearly all cases, if I believe a bet can convince an opponent to fold a better hand, I'll bet if my hand improves.

My Hand: 6♠ 5♠	The Flop: A♦ 7♣ 6♦	The Turn: 5♦

A bet here might convince my opponent to fold a bigger two pair.

♥ If I have the best hand possible after the turn, I plan to get as many chips into the pot as my opponents will allow. I think, "How can I get my opponent to make the biggest mistake possible?"

♥ In almost all cases when I improve my hand to two pair and when two pair is likely the best hand, I play extremely aggressively. My hand is very, very unlikely to improve on the river, while my opponent will very often be drawing live.

My Hand: A-J	The Flop: A-Q-4	The Turn: J
My Hand: 5-4	The Flop: K-5-2	The Turn: 4

When I turn two pair, I try to win the pot immediately, especially if I'm facing more than one opponent.

♥ If I've improved my hand and made a straight, I'll almost always try to bet and take the pot if there is a flush draw out against me. Bets of at least two thirds of the pot are appropriate. If there are no flush draws, having a straight can be very deceptive. If I've made a deceptive straight, going for a check-raise is usually appropriate.

♥ If I've improved my hand to a flush, I have the nut flush, and the board is unpaired, my opponent can, at best, be drawing to ten outs. They are about 20% to win in that case. Bets of one half the pot will give them three to one on their money when they are at best, 20% to make a full house on the river.

| My Hand: A♦ 5♦ | The Flop: K♦ Q♦ 4♣ | The Turn: 6♦ |

♥ If I do not have the nut flush and my opponent has a higher flush card, they have seven outs. They will make a winning hand about 14% of the time. But they are very likely to chase in this circumstance, if presented with a moderately sized bet. About half the pot will give them three to one on their money and will usually get called when they are taking away the worst of it.

♥ If I've improved my hand to a full house and I believe my opponent is on a flush draw or straight draw, I'll almost always bet about a third of the pot. My opponent will see that they are getting 4-1 on their money and think that they have about a 20% chance to get there even though they are drawing dead. I want them to think they are getting the right pot odds to call. Many players make a mistake by checking here, hoping that their opponents will make a flush or straight. I bet and give my opponents the right odds to chase that flush and straight. If I think they made their hand on the river, I'll always just bet right into them—a big bet—because I know I'll get called or raised.

WHEN A SCARE CARD HITS

A scare card is a card that comes on the turn that is very likely to scare players in the pot who had a good, but not great, hand after the flop.

If I've taken the lead in the betting after the flop and a scare card hits, I believe it is very often correct to relinquish the lead to my opponents. If they bet into me, I will usually just call. If they check to me, I will usually just check. In my experience players tend to go for too many check-raises in this situation. I will not oblige them with a bet. My goal is to play as small a pot as possible, even if it means that I give my opponent a free river card. Remember, a free river card is usually only going to hurt me about 20% of the time. I give up 20% equity in order to avoid committing chips to the pot when my opponent is very likely to be able to raise me out. Check-call is appropriate unless I have a fantastic read and can put my opponent on a draw.

If my opponent has the lead in the betting after the flop or displays any weakness after the flop and a scare card hits the turn, I'm very likely to go after the pot and apply significant pressure if my opponent displays any weakness whatsoever.

I try to remember that my opponents are doing their best to put me on a hand. If, in their estimation, the scare card could have helped me, I'll very often make a move that confirms their suspicions.

I've found that many players will bet a weak hand after a scare card hits that doesn't help their hand. Likewise, those same players are very likely to try to check-raise when the scare card hits their hand.

CALLING WITH A DRAW

With only one card to come, draws have very little value if my opponents are betting appropriately. With a flush draw or a straight draw, I'm only going to make my hand about 16–18% of the time. Almost any normal-size bet will not give me the right odds to continue.

The implied odds are the most important factor to consider when I'm deciding to call a bet with a draw after the turn card.

♠ If my opponent is in the habit of calling big bets on the river, I am more likely to play.
♠ If I believe my opponent is very strong but my draw

will make me even stronger, I'm more likely to play.

- ♠ If our stacks are very deep, I'm more likely to play.
- ♠ If my hand is at all deceptive (double gut-shot straight draws are the best), I'm more likely to play.
- ♠ If my draw has been telegraphed in any way, I'm more likely to fold, as my implied odds will be very small.
- ♠ If my opponent is an expert, I'm more likely to fold. Experts will often have a very good read on my hand at this point and they are very unlikely to pay me off if I hit my hand.

SEMIBLUFFING

After the turn I simply cannot afford to employ the strategy of betting my good hands and checking my bad hands. I must mix my strategy or even the simplest opponents will get the best of me. The best way to ensure a mixed strategy is to employ a tactic known as the semibluff.

A semibluff is a bet that is made with a hand that isn't likely to be the best hand but that has a chance to make the best hand on the river. Simply stated, a semibluff gives me two ways to win: Either I may make the best hand, or my opponent may fold. Semibluffing is an aggressive move that forces my opponents to make decisions. Occasionally, they'll make the wrong decisions and I will profit from their mistakes.

I've found that semibluffing works best if my opponent shows weakness either on the flop or after the turn. I seize on that weakness and hope to semibluff my way into taking the chips. If my opponent happens to call, at least I have some outs and can win by hitting my draw on the river.

Here are some factors that lead me to make a semibluff:

♦ The turn card gave me additional outs.
♦ My opponent showed weakness after the flop or after the turn—a semibluff is more likely to take the pot without confrontation.
♦ The turn card could have conceivably given me a better hand than my opponent has.
♦ My opponent is not a habitual check-raiser.
♦ My opponent is nowhere near pot committed.
♦ If I make the semibluff, I won't be pot committed.
♦ I can bet enough to force my opponent to make a critical decision—I very rarely semibluff when short stacked.
♦ Most of the hands I've recently had to showdown have been the best hands.

♦ My opponent does not make a habit of calling without appropriate odds. If I semibluff and my opponent is on a draw, they will call, and I'll have to fire yet another bullet after the river. This can be very scary.

TAKING DOWN THE POT

If the pot has a significant amount of money in it and I believe I have the best (albeit vulnerable) hand, I will very often overbet the pot in an attempt to take it down right away.

In a tournament any pot with at least half of an average stack is ripe for a big move—adding those chips to my stack without additional risk is worth giving away some post-turn equity, in most cases. This is especially true if taking down the pot will make me one of the chip leaders or give me a greater chance of moving up the money list.

If my hand is unlikely to improve and I think I have the best hand, I am very likely to make a big move at the pot. Straights and flushes when the board is paired and one pair when the board is flushing or straightening are both vulnerable hands. Small overpairs to the board are exceptionally vulnerable (T-T, Board 9-5-3-2).

Against very deceptive or skilled opponents, taking down the pot after the turn is good practice. Good players can use a scary river card to put me in a serious fix.

AFTER THE RIVER

By the time the river card is dealt, I usually have a very good indication of where I stand and what cards my opponents hold.

There is a lot of information at my disposal. My opponents have spoken volumes with their preflop actions, their postflop actions, their postturn actions, and any tells they've displayed in the few minutes since this hand started.

Good players will often be able to "read" through the backs of the cards and, by the time the river comes around, will have deduced an opponent's exact starting hand with startling accuracy. This is a skill I am always working on at the table. Even if I'm not involved in a particular hand, I will mentally work through the hand and venture a guess at the actual cards before the showdown. Getting it right will give me confidence when I get involved in a pot against those opponents later in the session. If I'm wrong, I'm apt to learn something very valuable.

Successful hand reading is, for most of us, an acquired skill that requires patience, intense focus and concentration, and dedicated practice. But the rewards are many. Great hand readers are rarely faced with a difficult decision after the river: It's tough to make a mistake when you know exactly what your opponent has.

When someone who has been playing a hand very weakly suddenly comes to life on the river and makes a big bet that smells fishy, I sense a bluff.

When someone who has been playing a hand very aggressively gets timid after the river card, I sense a trap.

When someone has played both aggressively and tentatively, I sense insecurity. They probably have a medium-strength hand.

If a player—especially a good player—bets after a river card that couldn't have helped his hand, I am apt to put him on a bluff. Good players don't bet medium-strength hands on the river.

GETTING PAID WITH
THE NUTS

If after the river card is dealt I have the nuts or near to it, I want to get paid off.

Some excellent players nearly always "value bet" with the nuts on the river, wagering slightly less than the "price" they think their opponent will call. While this is a sound strategy, I believe that most value bets are a little too easy to read for what they are.

I use an averaging method that makes me a little more unpredictable than the average value bettor. Once I've decided how much my opponent is likely to pay to see my hand, I plot a bell curve around their price. Sometimes I'll bet a little more, sometimes a little less.

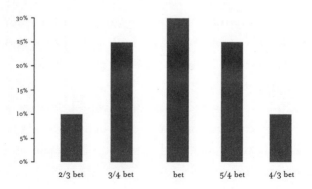

If I get called every time, I'll wind up making exactly as much as I would have if I had bet my opponent's exact price every time. But it will be much more difficult for my opponent to judge the strength of my hand. More important, my value bets don't look like value bets. My opponent can never really be sure what I have. That is a worthy goal, to be sure.

BETTING MEDIUM-STRENGTH HANDS

Players who are out of position and bet medium-strength hands after the river are making one of the worst mistakes in No Limit Hold'em, because:

1. They will usually get called only by a hand that beats them.
2. Their opponent will almost always fold a hand that can be beaten.
3. By committing chips to the pot voluntarily, they don't have a chance to save chips if their opponent checks a winning hand.
4. They lose the chance to induce an opponent to bluff.

The only really effective times to bet a hand out of position on the river are when I have a strong hand and want a call or a very weak hand that can't win unless my opponent folds.

If I have a weak or medium-strength hand but believe that my opponent's hand is even weaker, I've found that I win much more money by checking to him and trying to induce a bluff. I might then be faced with a difficult call, but that is poker. This is a very rare instance in No Limit Hold'em when I believe the check-call is not only valuable but a necessity.

If I am in position and my opponent checks to me after the river, I will dig deep and do my best to piece together the entire story. If my opponent has displayed weakness before the flop, after the flop, or after the turn, I will very often bluff on the river with a hand that cannot win without a bet.

When I have a medium-strength hand but don't have a great read on my opponent, I've found the best play is to check if he checks to me.

I am more likely to bet the river if the river card helped my hand or is a scare card for my opponent.

Against a good opponent who tends to check his medium-strength hand on the river, I am much less likely to bluff if he checks to me.

Here is an example from a tournament I played online recently at FullTiltPoker.com:

Blinds:	$25/$50
Average Stack:	$2,000
Players remaining:	120
My Stack:	$2,000 (40 big blinds)

I was in middle position with A♦ Q♦. Everyone folded to me, and I raised to $150, three times the big blind. Everyone folded to the button, a player I knew very little about, who called. The blinds folded.

The flop came down Q♣ 9♣ 2♣, a good flop for me. I led at the pot with a bet of $150. My opponent called.

The turn came K♦. I was worried about the straight draw and A-K, so I checked. My opponent checked. I put him on either a flush draw or A-9.

The river came 9♦, not a good river card. I felt like my hand was, at best, a medium-strength hand. I checked and my opponent bet $300. I called. He had J♣ 8♣, a busted flush draw with a gut shot, and I took the pot.

If I had bet, he definitely would have folded—and I would have won $300 less. If I had bet and he'd had a nine, I would have lost at least $300, and probably more.

BET OR CHECK-RAISE

The river card arrives and I think—or, better yet, *know*—that I've got the best hand. Now the key is to extract as much money from my opponent as possible. The question in front of me, if I'm first to act, is whether to bet or to check in the hopes of check-raising.

I ask the following questions:

♣ Was the river card scary for my opponent? If so, I'm not going to risk checking—I'm going to bet out. An innocuous river card makes me much more likely to check-raise.

♣ Was my opponent on a draw that missed? If so, I'm much more likely to check-raise. If I bet, he is not going to be able to put any money into the pot. If I check, he might take a stab at a bluff.

♣ Is my opponent very aggressive or tentative? If he is aggressive, I will check-raise more often.

♣ Does my opponent think he has the best hand and that it's good enough to bet if I check? If yes, this is a great time to check-raise. If no, I bet.

♣ Can my opponent afford to make a bet on the river if I check? If he'll be happy just to win the pot as it currently exists, I'll make a bet. If he still has plenty of chips and might be inclined to build a bigger pot, I'm more likely to check-raise.

♣ Is my opponent likely to pay off a check-raise? If no, I just go ahead and bet. I'll often win more money by overbetting the pot after the river than by check-raising and forcing my opponent to fold after he bets one half or three quarters of the pot.

♣ Have I check-raised on this hand so far? If so, I almost never go for the check-raise again. I'll just bet right out.

Because I almost never bet medium-strength hands on the river, my opponents will be less likely to fall for the check-raise. They should suspect either that I am very strong (and going for the check-raise) or that I have a very weak hand that won't be able to call a bet anyway.

Many inexperienced players overuse the check-raise on the river. Rare are the circumstances where the check-raise gains more than just betting right out. I estimate that I use the check-raise on the river less than one out of ten times the play is available to me.

TELLS

A flick of the wrist, a sideways glance. A shaking head, trembling hands. A lean back in the chair or a soulful, nearly inaudible moan. An act of strength, a purposeful display of weakness. For a professional poker player these are all tells that provide clues to an opponent's hand.

Tells come in two flavors. Involuntary tells are unconscious physical mannerisms that give away the strength or weakness of a hand. There are many, some more reliable than others. Observant poker players look for changes in posture, speech, intensity, and more.

The second form of tells is voluntary. Your opponent

will occasionally act one way because his hand is of the opposite type. They try to seem strong when they are weak and weak when they are strong, in a feeble attempt to manipulate the table. Great poker players don't fall for the act. A great poker player will sense when an opponent is playing a role, quickly determine the result the actor hopes to elicit, and then do exactly the opposite.

In this section I present some obvious and not-so-obvious tells. I wish I could take credit for figuring these out myself, but alas, most of them have been around a very long time. I read Mike Caro's seminal work on the topic, *Caro's Book of Poker Tells*, early in my poker education, and it changed the way I played the game. Many of my own observations are merely minor variations on themes covered by Mike nearly twenty years ago.

Although I am always observing the table in the hopes of finding tells, I might change only one in twenty decisions at the table when I think I've uncovered one. I find the cards, the situation, and the player to be far more reliable guides than tells are.

Still, observant players well versed in the psychology of tells will lose less money when they have the worst hand and win more money when they have the best. And that, dear reader, is what separates the good players from the great ones.

CARO'S GREAT LAW OF TELLS

In *Caro's Book of Poker Tells: The Psychology and Body Language of Poker*, author Mike Caro writes:

> Players are either acting or they aren't. If they are acting, then decide what they want you to do and disappoint them.

Players who are acting weak are usually strong. They want me to put money into the pot. I disappoint them by checking or folding.

Players who are acting strong are generally weak. They want me to fold or check. I disappoint them with a bet or a raise.

Many, many tells are a variation on this weak equals strong, strong equals weak theme.

BEWARE OF THE SPEECH

Here's a lesson I learned (the easy way, as it turns out) early in my tournament career. I raised before the flop with pocket kings, causing everybody to fold except the big blind, a loose player who re-raised me. Undaunted, I re-raised right back at him, committing about a third of my chips to the pot.

The big blind rose from his chair, looked at no one in particular, and said something along the lines of, "Well, I guess I gotta do what I gotta do. . . . It's alright, I've been wanting to see that new movie with Harrison Ford. Or maybe I'll enter a satellite for the big one. . . . Ah, hell, I'm all-in."

I called.

The big blind, as I should have expected, turned up pocket aces. My goose should have been cooked.

Fate turned out to have other plans for me that day. I sucked out a king on the flop and busted the guy, sending him straight to the movie theater and the bomb *Six Days, Seven Nights.*

The legendary T. J. Cloutier happened to be sitting at the same table. A few seconds after the guy was out of earshot, T. J. turned to me and said, "Boy, haven't you heard the expression 'Beware of the speech'? You've got a few things to learn."

Any time someone at the table goes out of his way to give a speech before he raises, I do my best to get out of the way. Just about every single time I've disregarded

T. J.'s advice, my opponent has turned over the immortal nuts.

VARIED BET SIZES

I look for players who give away the strength of their hand by varying the size of their bet before the flop. Some players will raise two times the blind when they have a good hand and four times the blind when they are trying to steal. Others will do the opposite. When I figure out which strategy a player is using, I will bet and reraise to exploit that tell.

THE OUT-OF-TURN BET

In the *World Series of Poker* championship event a few years back, a very solid but inexperienced player sat to my immediate right. During the four hours or so we'd been at the same table, I observed that he, too, was watching each hand intently, playing tight-aggressive poker. I was impressed.

It was the middle of the second day, and the blinds had increased to the size where stealing them became a necessity. Protecting one's own blinds and "re-stealing" were even more important.

I was in the big blind. Everyone had folded to the button, who seemed to be debating his actions. Before he could decide, however, the observant player on my right declared "Raise!" and tossed in a bet four times the size of the big blind!

The dealer, enforcing the rules, politely told the small blind he was acting out of turn and returned his bet.

Now the button was in a fix. Clearly, he didn't want to attempt a steal-raise when the small blind seemed to have such a big hand. He decided to fold. Finally his turn to act, the small blind made the same large raise, four times the big blind.

Something triggered an alarm in my head. Why in the world would this guy bet out of turn? He had been watching the action intently all day and hadn't once bet out of turn.

Well, it didn't take me more than a second to figure out that my opponent was acting to disguise what must be a weak hand. I re-raised. My obviously disgusted opponent mucked his hand, and I picked up a decent-size pot without even having to look at my cards.

When a player raises out of turn, I ask myself if it might have been intentional. If so, the raiser is most likely very weak.

BIG CHIPS, SMALL CHIPS

Not so long ago I found myself playing in a fairly big No Limit game. The table was shorthanded—only five players—but the $25/$25 blinds helped to generate pots in the thousands of dollars. We were using two denominations to place our bets, green $25 chips and black $100 chips.

Finding A-9 offsuit under the gun, I decided to make what had become the standard raise to $75. The guy on my left counted out $300—three black chips—and re-raised. I folded.

A few hands later I found A-T under the gun, and once again raised to $75. The guy on my left counted out $300—twelve green chips—and re-raised.

Why would a guy raise with black chips one time and green chips the next? I thought about it for a minute or so.

I decided two things: first, the black chips seemed

more valuable than the green and thus less expendable; and second, twelve chips were meant to look more intimidating than three.

Perhaps he had been inviting me to call with the black-chip raise, meaning, of course, that he had a very good hand. With the twelve green chips, on the other hand, not only was he attempting to portray strength—a sure sign of weakness—but he was using "less valuable" chips that were more expendable.

I decided that the green-chip raise represented a bluff and re-raised him. He folded! His tell allowed me, over the course of the next couple of hours, to pick off his raises without mercy until I had broken him.

The Weakness=Strength/Strength=Weakness tell manifests in many ways at the table.

CHIP STACKS

Neatly organized stacks of chips are usually the sign of a player who doesn't like to gamble. Alternatively, haphazardly arranged chips generally hint that their owner is a looser player willing to mix it up.

Many players will count out their session's winnings, placing them in a separate stack. When I see an opponent do that, I do my best to break that barrier. I can take this to an extreme at times, but it seems to work for me.

A few years back I was in a game against a tight "rock" of a player. He had pushed his initial $5,000 buy-in up to $7,200, arranging the $2,200 profit in a separate pile. It occurred to me that he'd be very unlikely to invest more than that $2,200 unless he had a great hand, a tendency I might be able to exploit.

I got my chance after I missed a draw in a pot in which we'd each invested about $1,000. When he checked to me on the river, I looked at the $1,200 he had remaining in his "profit pile" . . . and proceeded to bluff $1,400 at the pot.

He looked long and hard at the $1,200 in that pile, but finally decided to fold. To this day, I believe that if I had bet $1,200 or less, he would have called in a heartbeat. Many players become very apprehensive when faced with a decision that could turn a winning session into a losing one.

WHEN THEY'RE BUSY,
THEY'RE TIGHT

When my opponents at the table are busy with activities unrelated to the game at hand, I try to give them something extra to think about. I find that they are far more likely to fold or play suboptimally when they are preoccupied.

By "busy," I mean:

♥ Stacking a lot of chips or counting a lot of bills after winning a big pot
♥ Dealing with a chip runner for a rebuy or add-on
♥ Taking a cell-phone call
♥ Changing the tunes on their music player
♥ Having a friend come over to say hello
♥ Talking to someone else at the table
♥ Getting a delivery from the cocktail server or food server

On the other hand, when a busy opponent makes a big bet, I will approach the situation with extreme caution. He will generally have a very big hand.

SUIT CHECK

When the flop comes with three cards of the same suit and an opponent double-checks their hole cards, they very often have one of that suit. If they raise with big slick before the flop, they know that they have A-K. They know that one is a diamond and one is a club, but they can't remember which is which. They have to recheck after the flop.

I have almost never seen a player with a made flush do a double take in that spot.

QUICK BET, SLOW BET

Here's another variation of the strength/weakness tell. Opponents who bet quickly tend to have weaker hands than opponents who bet slowly. A quick bet is meant to intimidate, the speed a substitute for real strength. A slow bet, on the other hand, is meant to imply uncertainty.

CHANGES IN DEMEANOR

When talkative players suddenly become silent, I find that they usually have a hand they intend to play.

When players who usually slouch in their chair suddenly straighten up, they're usually going to play.

When players who are eating at the table look at their cards and put their forks down, I find that they usually have a hand they intend to play.

If a player's phone rings during a hand and they don't make some sort of move to answer it, they are generally committed to playing the hand. If they answer the phone, even to tell the caller to hold on for a minute, they are usually weak.

LEANERS AND SLOUCHERS

I've found that players who sit up and lean over the table usually have weak hands. Players who slouch or lean backward in their chairs usually have strong hands. The leaners are getting close to the action in an effort to intimidate. The slouchers are trying to act as nonconfrontational as possible.

SHAKY HANDS

A player whose hand shakes when putting their chips into the pot is *usually* holding a very strong hand.

There are, however, exceptions to the rule. In 2003 I was playing in a pretty big No Limit game at Hank Azaria's house in Hollywood, against players who were mostly unfamiliar to me. Finding pocket jacks on the cutoff, I decided to raise an early limper. Everyone folded back to the limper, who with very shaky hands moved all of his chips into the middle.

I tossed my jacks faceup into the middle to show everyone what a great laydown I had made, adding, "Man, with hands shaking that bad I would have folded queens! If you don't have aces, I'd be very surprised."

His hands were still shaking as he turned over his pocket fives. "You fell for the shaky hand tell," announced Hank. "Don't pay any attention to that—he's a recovering alcoholic." I later found out that the limper had a nickname: "Shakes."

WHEN THEY LOOK AT THEIR CHIPS

Here's a very reliable tell that usually occurs right after the flop, turn, or river card has been dealt. When a new card helps an opponent's hand, they will often glance down at their stack for a split second.

I can almost read their mind. "Oooh! What a card! I'm going to bet. . . . Where are those chips again? Oh yeah, right below my nose. . . ."

WHEN THEY LOOK AT MY CHIPS

When my opponents eye my stack, they are usually visualizing what my chips will look like in their own stack. These players are telling me that they have a good hand and they know (or think) I'm weak.

If I happen to observe this tell when I'm holding a very powerful hand, I will often overbet the pot or attempt a check-raise.

THE QUICK CALL

I've found that players who call very quickly after the flop usually have a drawing hand.

Think about it this way: If they had a very good hand, they would have to give some consideration (and time) to raising. If they had a very bad or marginal hand, they would have to give some consideration (and time) to folding. Only when they have a drawing hand does calling become nearly automatic.

THE SLOW CALL

I've found that players who take a long time to call a bet after the flop are usually considering raising or folding. They either have a very strong hand or a moderately weak hand. Very rarely will they be on a pure straight or flush draw.

WHEN THEY REACH FOR THEIR CHIPS

When I am considering betting or raising and my opponent reaches for their chips while I'm thinking, I will almost always fire a bet. They are acting in the hopes of convincing me not to bet and, per Mike Caro's advice, I am going to disappoint them.

TOSS VS. SLIDE

Players who toss their chips haphazardly into the pot are usually weak, overcompensating for a lack of strength with an overly flamboyant betting style.

Players who smoothly and effortlessly slide their chips into the pot are trying to make their bet as easy to call as possible. Think strong.

The combination move of sliding the chips into the pot then leaning back in the chair is almost a sure sign of a great hand.

REVERSE TELLS

In 2002 I was playing in a big No Limit tournament in Reno and had reached the middle levels with a slightly above-average stack. Young Pham, a very bright, fantastic player, sat on my left. Young was short stacked, having recently taken a very bad beat that left him with only five big blinds or so.

Everyone folded to me in the small blind, where I looked down to find J-7 suited. Not a great hand, but with my larger stack and the antes in play, I gave serious thought to putting Young all-in. He couldn't hurt me much, and even against a hand like A-T, I'd be getting just about the right pot odds to take the chance. But I don't like to double up the short stack with a trashy hand, especially with an opponent as dangerous as Young.

Unsure how to proceed, I reached for my chips to try to pick up a tell from Young. He instantly reached for his chips. "Aha!" I thought. "That's a classic tell. He doesn't want me to raise!" Hoping to disappoint him, I raised him all-in.

Young nearly beat me to the pot, flipping over K-K with an oh-so-polite wink.

Great players will, at times, reverse the traditional meaning of an action if they think I'm paying attention. The truly great players set up plays, revealing some tell for four or five pots, then reversing it to win a big one.

TOURNAMENT STRATEGIES

No Limit Hold'em tournaments are all the rage. The multi-million-dollar prize purses in professional poker far surpass those of any other sport. The *World Series of Poker*, the *World Poker Tour*—these tournaments have captured the world's attention and driven millions of new players to the game.

I don't play many cash games. I focus primarily on tournaments, the biggest tournaments in the world. Just a few years ago there was only one $10,000 buy-in tournament: the *World Series of Poker* championship event. Now it seems like there's a $10,000 buy-in tournament every week. A big field used to include maybe 200 players.

Today's fields routinely exceed 1,000 players. The biggest tournament to date—the 2005 *World Series of Poker* championship event—attracted a record 6,600 players, creating a prize purse in excess of $65,000,000. There is no doubt in my mind that very soon that number will again be eclipsed.

I prefer tournament play because it requires a constantly changing strategy. It's not unlike television's *Survivor*, where contestants are urged to "Outwit. Outplay. Outlast." Only, tournament poker requires "Outdraw" as well.

In cash games I'm never short stacked, never the big stack, never facing a "bubble," never holding on for dear life when looking at elimination. Tournaments require discipline. I can't get up and leave if things go badly, I can't change tables, and I can't magically materialize more chips in my stack if I make a bonehead play. Oh yeah, and then there are those multimillion dollar prizes. . . .

I find it very interesting that there are some absolutely terrific No Limit cash game players who suffer miserable results in tournaments. Likewise, there are some incredibly talented tournament players who are dead money in the cash games. The two styles of play, while similar, require very different sets of skills. Both can be very rewarding when played well, but for me, tournament poker is the nuts.

STAYING ALIVE

Tournaments are about survival. Doubling up early means much less regarding your chances of winning than doubling up with just a few tables remaining. The fewer fifty-fifty chances I take, especially early in a tournament, the better off I am.

BUILD A TIGHT IMAGE EARLY

I've found very tight play—squeaky-tight, some might say—during the first two or three stages of a tournament to be very valuable:

- ♣ I build a great image as a tight player, and I'm able to exploit this image when the blinds go up.
- ♣ I don't risk losing a lot of chips with weak hands.
- ♣ The blinds really are too small to be worth stealing.
- ♣ I have a chance to sit back and watch, profiling players and picking up their tells before I have to get involved in a pot and make big decisions against them.

WHEN THE POT IS BIG

When the pot gets big—say half the size of the average stack—and I think I have the best hand, I will very often push all-in and try to take the pot right away. I may be losing the chance to milk the pot for a little more expectation, but, if successful, I won't have to risk an opponent drawing out on me, no matter how slim the chances.

In war, then, your great object is victory,
not lengthy campaigns.
—Sun Tzu, *The Art of War*

TAKE A TIME-OUT AFTER
SIGNIFICANT CHANGES

Just before play started at the final table of the *World Series of Poker* championship event in 2001, I asked Chris Ferguson—the 2000 world champion—for a bit of advice. I'll never forget what he told me, as it has helped me immensely ever since: Any time there is a significant change, take a few minutes to figure out how the dynamics of the table have been affected.

Take a "time-out" when:

♠ A player just won a big pot.
♠ A player just lost a big pot.
♠ A player at the table just got caught bluffing.
♠ A player was just eliminated.
♠ A player is tilting.
♠ A player has likely changed gears for some reason.
♠ The blinds have been increased.

During my time-out, here are some of the things I think about:

♦ Should I be more passive or more aggressive?
♦ How has my image changed?
♦ Who may be on tilt?
♦ Should I change gears?
♦ Is the payout structure a consideration?

KNOW THEIR STACK SIZE

I constantly keep track of the stack size of every player at my table. Throughout a hand I remain very aware of my opponents' position relative to the average stack, my stack, and the other stacks at the table and the tournament.

I've also found it useful to keep track of my opponents' "high-water marks." Some players will stretch to call if winning will allow them to pass a threshold they have not yet reached in the tournament.

GET LUCKY . . . AT THE RIGHT TIME

"Your mission is to put yourself in a position to get lucky."
—Tom McEvoy, 1983 *World Series of Poker* champion and noted author

TARGET THE AVERAGE STACKS

When I first started playing tournaments, I was constantly told to "go after the short stacks."

Like the good boy I am, I did as I was told. In the middle and late stages of a tournament, I would raise the short stacks with substandard hands in an effort to bust them. What I discovered in nearly every instance is that these short stacks, having decided they were pot committed, were going to call or make a play at me. By trying to bust the short stack, I very often had my money in the pot without the best hand.

At my very first *World Series of Poker* championship event, I was fortunate enough to have a beer with one of the greatest No Limit players in the game, Layne "Back-to-Back" Flack. In the five minutes it took to order the beer, Layne managed to completely transform my thinking.

"Phil, going after the short stacks is just wrong thinking. They are desperate and have to take chances. In a tournament I'm often targeting the *average* stacks. They can afford to fold. They can afford to make a big laydown. I do my best to stay out of the way of the big stacks and the small stacks unless I have a premium hand."

Layne, undoubtedly following his own advice, went on to win two No Limit Hold'em *World Series of Poker* bracelets the following year, thus earning his nickname.

PLAY SMALL POCKET PAIRS

There aren't too many feelings in No Limit Hold'em that are better than when you flop a set. It is one of the only times in the game when I am nearly certain that I have the best hand.

I've found that in tournaments most of the value offered by small pocket pairs comes from the implied odds of flopping a set against a good or great hand. When I have 7-7 and the flop comes a rainbow K-7-2, I'm dreaming of busting a guy with A-K.

Almost anytime I have more than forty big blinds, I'll call up to five big blinds in order to see a flop when I have a pocket pair.

DON'T GO BROKE WITH ONE PAIR

It's a prominent feature in many bad-beat stories. "I raised with pocket kings on the button and the small blind called. The flop came down J-8-2 with three suits, the guy bet, so I moved in on him. He turns over pocket deuces, and I'm drawing almost stone cold dead!"

I like to be the guy with pocket twos, not the guy with pocket kings. Yes, overpairs to the board are great hands, but how good can one pair be if my opponent is willing to put all his chips in the pot?

Very often the guy who flops the set against me will check-raise. When I get check-raised and have an overpair to the board, I will think long and hard before calling.

Against a set, I am drawing nearly dead to two outs. I'm a twelve to one underdog after the flop and a twenty-two to one underdog after the turn. I've got about the same chance of making a runner-runner flush!

When I have only an overpair to the board, I do my best to play a very small pot.

To secure ourselves against defeat lies in our own hands, but the opportunity of defeating the enemy is provided by the enemy himself.
—Sun Tzu, *The Art of War*

SAMPLE TOURNAMENT PAYOUT STRUCTURE

Most tournaments pay around 30% of the prize pool for first place. I am in favor of very flat payout structures, especially with very large fields.

Here is a very flat payout structure from a tournament at FullTiltPoker.com:

Prize Pool: $50,000 (500 entrants, $100/player)

Place	Money	% of Pool
1	$12,500	25.00%
2	$7,750	15.50%
3	$5,625	11.25%
4	$4,375	8.75%
5	$3,250	6.50%
6	$2,375	4.75%
7	$1,650	3.30%
8	$1,250	2.50%
9	$875	1.75%
10–12	$550	1.10%
13–15	$400	0.80%
16–18	$325	0.65%
19–27	$250	0.50%
28–36	$200	0.40%
37–45	$150	0.30%
46–54	$125	0.25%

PLAYING TO WIN
TOURNAMENTS

I almost always play to win. Titles, bracelets, and the glory of winning are the most important things for me. As a result I sometimes make decisions that would be considered suboptimal in a cash game.

Players who "play to survive" can be manipulated. They are, for example, much easier to bluff, as their primary goal is not to get knocked out of the tournament.

Players who are playing to move up the money ladder can also be manipulated. Very often these opponents will play too tight.

Mathematicians tell me that playing for the highest equity is the right thing to do in tournaments, but I just can't bring myself to do it. I am there to win. Not to win the most money, but to win the title. Each player has his or her own goals in a tournament, and it is one's duty to devise a strategy that will maximize the chance of reaching those goals.

MONEY MEANS SOMETHING

In most tournaments everyone who has survived to see the final table is going to see some prize money. But the amount depends on where you finish. With each player eliminated, the prize money gets bigger. The difference between spots can often be measured in the hundreds of thousands, even millions, of dollars.

When I get to the final table, I make a mental note of players who are looking to move up a few spots. There are always a few players who have decided they "need the money" and will play tight enough to get the payday they desire. A guy who owes $24,000 on his credit card isn't going to risk going out in eighth place and receiving $17,000 when he can just fold his way out of debt.

There is very often an artificial bubble created when the prize purses go from five digits to six digits. It's like buying a book for $19.95. That seems a lot easier to take than a book that lists for $20.00. Similarly, $103,000 sounds like a lot more money than $95,000.

A player who is looking to move up—as opposed to playing to win—is going to take fewer chances with his chips, providing all kinds of opportunities to an opponent who is willing to take the bigger risks.

MAKING A DEAL

The practice of cutting deals in tournaments is both common and (usually) straightforward. It is almost inevitable that at some point during the final table someone will propose a way to split the prize money and the title in order to take some of the risk out of future play.

I find that making deals (for me, anyway) is usually bad policy. If an opponent is badly in need of the money, he is likely to be playing a suboptimal game in an effort to move up the prize ladder. The mental energy I have to expend evaluating a potential deal is energy that I can't focus on the game. And as most players are relatively inexperienced at playing shorthanded tables, I find that my own experience gives me an edge that is unlikely to be reflected in whatever deal is being floated.

That being said, I have made deals in the past, and I will probably make deals in the future.

Since most of the prize money in tournaments is divided between first and second place, here is an easy formula I use for figuring out an equitable split when I get heads-up: Each player is awarded second place money. Whatever money remains in the prize pool gets divided by chip count.

For example, say there are only two players remaining. Player A has $10,000 to Player B's $5,000. First prize pays $20,000 and second pays $10,000.

Both players would get the second place money—$10,000—leaving another $10,000 in the prize pool. Player A gets two thirds of that money (he has two thirds of the chips) and Player B takes the remaining one third. In other words, Player A receives a total of $16,666, while Player B takes $13,334.

STEAL THE BLINDS!

Stealing the blinds is an absolutely crucial element to my tournament success. My aim, assuming an average or above-average stack in the middle and late stages of a tournament, is to steal the blinds 1.3 times per orbit (or, for the haters of decimals, four times every three orbits).

Consider this example:

Blinds are $500/$1,000 with $200 antes for the next two hours, until they go up to $600/$1,200 with $200 antes. I have $40,000 in chips, or forty big bets.

There are nine players at my table, where we are averaging four "orbits," or thirty-six hands per hour.

Under these conditions, each pot contains $3,300 in blinds and antes before any action is taken. It's going to cost me $3,300 an orbit—one ante for each of the nine hands, plus the small and big blinds—just to stay in the game.

Winning my "fair share"—one pot per orbit—will allow me to break even. But the point isn't to break even, but to grow my stack. By taking 1.3 pots each time around the table, I can increase my chips by $1,100 every orbit.

During the eight orbits I hope to see during this level, my thieving ways will net me $8,800.

The level ends and the blinds go up to $600/$1,200. I now have $48,800—a little more than forty big bets. While many other players have gone broke, I have stayed even with the increasing blinds and am well on my way to the final table.

Note that in tournaments with very fast structures (the blinds double every level) or shorter levels (the levels change every hour), I have to steal the blinds much more frequently to stay even.

Here is a table of next levels and the corresponding number of times I need to steal the blinds to have the same number of big bets:

Increases	Time Length of Level (in minutes)			
	30	60	90	120
20% increase	2.3	1.6	1.4	1.3
30% increase	2.8	1.9	1.6	1.5
40% increase	3.4	2.2	1.8	1.6
50% increase	4.0	2.5	2.0	1.8

If my goal is to remain even with the blinds and I am facing a 30% increase when the next level begins in sixty minutes, I need to steal the blinds 1.9 times per orbit.

I steal with a coldhearted larceny that will eventually lead to the final table. If I never see the river—or even a flop, for that matter—I can never receive a bad beat. There are no big suckouts and no big decisions.

Supreme excellence consists in breaking the
enemy's resistance without fighting.
—Sun Tzu, *The Art of War*

WHEN STEALING THE BLINDS
DOESN'T WORK

In the real world, stealing blinds can be a lot more
frustrating than it sounds. I have played in many tournaments where it seemed like every time I made a play for
a pot, someone would re-raise and force me to throw my
hand away.

When I find myself in one of these games or
tournaments, I have to adopt a different strategy. It
just so happens that the best way to fight back is to
adopt the same strategy that is frustrating me. If I can't
steal the blinds, then I will steal the raises in front of
me with well timed re-raises from the blinds or late
position.

It's a great way to keep my stack alive while moving
up toward the final table. I find that employing this

tactic one time every one-and-a-half orbits is enough to build my stack fast enough to thwart the ever increasing blinds.

Remember, a successful re-raise steal, assuming the initial raiser brings it in for three times the big blind, will net four-and-a-half big blinds plus the antes (usually equivalent to one big blind), or five-and-a-half big blinds.

After three orbits I will have paid seven-and-a-half big blinds in blinds and antes, but I will have won eleven big blinds from my two successful re-raise thefts. That's a net profit of three-and-a-half big blinds.

And just like stealing blinds, if I pick my spots carefully, there is no chance of suffering a bad beat—I can win all my pots before I have to see the flop.

I find that the easiest players to target are the ones who play too many hands. The absolutely ideal conditions for the re-raise steal occur when that loose player raises from middle to late position against blinds who play weak-tight.

Here is a table that I use to figure out how often I need to employ the re-raise steal technique to keep up with the increased stakes of the impending next level:

Increases	Time Length of Level (in minutes)			
	30	60	90	120
20% increase	1.2	0.85	0.75	0.70
30% increase	1.5	1.0	0.85	0.75
40% increase	1.8	1.15	0.95	0.85
50% increase	2.1	1.3	1.05	0.90

For example, if the stakes are increasing 30% in 60 minutes, I need to re-steal one time every orbit to stay even with the increase.

For online tournaments, I usually triple the length of the round to find the appropriate entry in the above table. Per hour online, I play about three times the number of hands that I play in a casino.

STEAL OR RE-RAISE?

So, which is the better strategy—stealing blinds or stealing raises?

Against a tight table, stealing the blinds is the best strategy.

Against a loose table, the re-raise steal is the best strategy.

KEEP THE AVERAGE STACK SIZE IN MIND

When I'm playing tournaments, I keep the average stack size in mind at all times. It's easy to calculate:

$$\text{Average} = \frac{\text{Total number of chips in play}}{\text{Number of players remaining}}$$

The size of the average stack doesn't affect too many of my decisions, but it does give me an indication as to where I stand in relation to the rest of the field. By comparing my stack and the average stack to the size of the blinds and antes, I can determine both how fast (or aggressively) I should play and how fast my opponents are likely to play.

Let's say I've reached the later stages of a tournament where the average stack size is about twenty to twenty-five big blinds. That's not a lot of room to work with. Nearly every player in the game will feel pressured, resulting in wilder, looser play. I can counter this trend, assuming my stack size allows it, by playing more conservatively.

If the opposite were true—for example, in the middle

stages where the average stack contains fifty to one hundred big blinds—then I could expect my opponents, who feel no pressure from the blinds and antes, to play a tighter game. Once again, I can run counter to the herd, in this case loosening my play.

In some online tournaments the rapidly increasing blind structure can create an average stack size of five to seven blinds or less! Players will feel compelled to raise all-in or fold. Nothing else makes much sense.

I also use the average stack size as a sort of clock to keep track of my competition. At the start of a tournament the average stack size is equal to the starting stack. When half the field has been eliminated, the average stack will be twice the original number of chips. When three quarters of the field has been eliminated, the average stack size will be four times the initial starting stack.

BE COMFORTABLE AT THIRTY BIG BETS

How many big blinds are enough?

I find that in tournament play thirty big blinds are

enough to allow me to play comfortably. With this many chips the blinds and antes aren't going to force me to spend more (on average) than 1% of my stack per hand. At this rate I can last somewhere in the neighborhood of five orbits (fifty hands, 50% of my stacks) before having to switch to short-stack play.

When I am in the thirty-big-blind "comfort zone," I almost never worry about the average stack size. I can focus on playing tight, aggressive poker. I can pick my spots. I don't have to rush to commit to the pot. I don't have to take chances. I don't have to make big plays. I can afford to lay down the best hand, and I can afford to go after the easy money if it feels right.

PLAYING THE BIG STACK

Being the big stack is extraordinarily fun.

It's amazing how much simpler No Limit Hold'em tournament play becomes when I have a big stack as opposed to an average or small stack. My options multiply. I can bully and attack. I can sit back and wait for my opponents to make a fatal mistake. The big stack is poker's ultimate luxury.

When I'm lucky enough to have a big stack, here are some of the aggressive changes that I make to my game:

♣ I never limp into the pot. Ever. The big stack gives me the license to apply extra pressure to my opponents. If I'm first in the pot, I always raise

♣ If the blinds are tight players with average stacks, I will play nearly every single hand when I'm late position or the button.

♣ When I think they are weak, I punish all limpers with big raises from position or the blinds.

♣ I call from position more often when an opponent with an average stack enters the pot with a raise. My big stack allows me to see more flops that have big implied odds. I don't, however, invest any more money into the pot if I don't hit the flop hard—chasing hands is the perfect way to lose that big stack and all of the options it affords me.

Not all of the changes I make to my game when I've got the big stack, however, involve aggression. In certain situations I will play more cautiously when I'm sitting on a large pile of chips:

♥ I will rarely, if ever, confront a short-stacked opponent without a premium hand. One of the fastest ways to go from a big stack to a medium or average stack is to try to bust short-stacked opponents with a bad hand. The best way to keep those short stacks short is to wait them out until I've been dealt a hand where I'm a favorite. Then I can apply maximum pressure.

♥ I try to win more pots before the flop. Stealing blinds and antes is the best way to maintain a big stack. I'm not looking for big confrontations. I'll be more than happy to "chip" my way through the field and to the final table with my big stack intact.

♥ If on the flop or the turn I think I have the best hand, I will often try to take the pot right away. The best way to keep a big stack is to grow it slowly. The worst way to lose a big stack is to give it away quickly.

Some very good players build big stacks and then go on absolute tears, betting and raising nearly every pot. That strategy has rarely been effective for me. If I'm fortunate enough to get a big stack, I want to keep it.

At the Bay 101 Shooting Star tournament in 2004, I made it to the six-handed final table with $1,238,000 in chips. My closest competitor, Masoud Shojaei, had $416,000. Given that four of my five opponents were very inexperienced in final-table play, I decided to wield my big stack like a club, raising aggressively in any spot I could find.

It turned out to be a remarkably ineffective strategy. Every time I raised before the flop, one of my opponents would come over the top of me with a re-raise.

My friend Rafe Furst, watching from the gallery, sent me a text message on my cell phone: "Dude, slow down, they are not giving your raises any respect. Grind them out with that big stack, bro, and let them come to you."

It was the perfect advice at the perfect time. I changed gears, buckled down, and waited patiently for better opportunities. Not until I felt I had sufficiently "rehabilitated" my image did I begin to steal some pots again.

We eventually got down to three-handed play, my big stack intact. With $1,300,000 in chips, I was able to get a little lucky and bust both of my remaining opponents, Masoud and 2003 *World Series of Poker* champion Chris Moneymaker, on the same hand. The victory not only earned me $360,000 but provided me with a memory I'll never forget.

WHEN THE ANTES START

Once I reach the level in a tournament where the antes kick in, I invariably find myself ready to change gears.

The antes at the *World Series of Poker* championship event begin at the fourth level. At this point I've been playing for six hours. I have built a tight image. I have a good idea of how my opponents like to play. I am ready to shed my squeaky-tight game and start aggressively stealing some blinds and antes.

Walk around at a big tournament a few hours after the antes have started. The best players in the room will have a disproportionate number of "ante chips" in front of them—they are the players who are stealing those antes and building their stacks.

SHORT STACKS

Playing a short stack requires a great deal of patience. Because I don't have many chips, the opportunity to play my hand is severely limited after the flop. I start to think "all-in or fold," and wait for a good situation to risk whatever chips I have left.

When I have thirteen to fifteen times the size of the big blind, I look for opportunities to re-raise all-in against a loose raiser with an average or slightly above-average stack. If I can get him to fold, I'll usually pick up a pot around the size of five or six big blinds.

When I have eight to eleven times the size of the big blind, I think about taking some more significant risks. I will raise all-in to steal blinds from average or medium-big stacks. I will re-raise all-in with any premium hand. I gladly accept fifty-fifty propositions with this stack size.

When I get down to four to six times the size of the big blind, I have only one move, and that move is all-in. If someone bets in front of me, I may have to call all-in with any pocket pair, an ace with a decent kicker, or any other hand that I think has about a fifty-fifty chance of winning.

SUPER SHORT STACK STRATEGY

More often than I'd like, I find myself with a *very* short stack, say one to two-and-a-half big blinds. And while this is not a pleasant position to be in, all is not lost.

Very early in my professional career I started the final table of a No Limit Hold'em tournament with $100. The average stack was more than $6,000. Guess who won.

In the 1982 *World Series of Poker* championship event, Jack "Treetop" Straus had already risen to leave the table when he discovered a single $500 chip tucked under the rail. He returned to his seat, resumed play, and won the championship, generating the now familiar poker adage "All you need is a chip and a chair."

While nobody likes to play from a supershort stack, it's an inevitable part of the game. There are several strategies that I believe provide me with the maximum chance of coming back from the ropes.

——IN THE BLINDS——

If I'm in the blind and more than half of my money is already in the pot, I will almost always go all-in without bothering to look at my hand. There are literally no two cards I could have that would make it correct to fold against a hand as powerful as A-K. I'll put the rest of my money into the middle and take my chances. I simply don't fold any hand preflop when I'm getting 3 to 1 on my money or more.

—IN EARLY POSITION—

With the big blind imminent I am looking for any above-average hand. I'll certainly push all-in with any pocket pair, any ace, any medium or bigger suited connectors, and just about any hand Q-7 or higher. If I find myself stuck with a worse-than-average hand, I'll fold and pray for something better in the big blind.

—IN MIDDLE POSITION—

If I'm the first in, I'll play any ace, any pocket pair, heck, I'll play anything that looks remotely above average. For me to call an early position bettor, however, I need a good reason: suited connectors, a pocket pair, or a big ace. I will *not* call all-in with a ragged ace—my chances of being completely dominated are too great. I would much prefer to call all-in with 9-8 suited than A-2 offsuit or K-9 offsuit. My goal is to get all of my chips into the middle with a hand that rates to be a "coin flip" or better against a single opponent.

—IN LATE POSITION—

If I'm the first into the pot, I'm looking for any good hand: a pocket pair, anything that adds up to twenty-one in blackjack. I have some time, so I'm not in a hurry to commit all my chips without a decent hand. My goal, as always, is to get all-in with the best hand.

In rare circumstances I have folded a good hand in late position, but only because there was a high likelihood that another player would go broke before I had to commit the rest of my chips. And the additional prize money for moving up a spot seemed significant.

It can be correct to fold marginally playable hands in late position very late in a tournament if another opponent has a high chance of going broke before I have to commit all my chips.

WAIT FOR THE BLINDS TO INCREASE

Since I only have one move with my supershort stack—all-in—why not wait until the blinds and antes are a little higher? If I'm nearing a change in level and have a choice between going all-in with a very marginal hand or waiting a hand for the blinds and antes to go up, I'll always wait for the new level. There will be more money in the pot when I eventually have to take a stand.

REBUYS AND ADD-ONS

Whenever I enter a tournament with rebuys, I am always ready to reopen my wallet and rebuy if I go broke.

If an available add-on offers a "chip overlay," it is always right to take it. For example, I once played in a tournament whose $100 entry fee netted me $1,000 in tournament chips. For another $100 at the end of the rebuy period, however, I could add on another $2,000 in tournament chips. That kind of overlay is a steal and thus absolutely mandatory no matter how many chips I have at the break.

If you're not afraid to reach back into your pockets, rebuys can allow you to play with reckless abandon. The $1,000 No Limit Hold'em event at the 2004 *World Series of Poker* offered rebuys and add-ons to its participants. No one took fuller advantage than Daniel Negreanu, who went broke a reported twenty-seven times during the rebuy period.

Having invested $28,000 into the tournament, whose 538 players made 534 rebuys and 262 add-ons, Daniel switched to his A-game once the rebuy period (mercifully) came to an end. He finished third, good for a $101,000 prize and a $73,000 profit on his investment.

Why would Daniel play like a maniac and go broke twenty-seven times? To build a big stack. There were many chips in play at Daniel's table (mostly due to his numerous rebuys!), and he managed to collect a very large number of them before the end of the rebuy period. These chips provided him with plenty of ammunition for the rest of the tournament.

I have heard another unconfirmed but entirely possible explanation for Daniel's strategy. He may have had a very large "last longer" side bet with another professional player in the tournament. Daniel decided that his best chance to win the bet would be to build the biggest stack he could during the rebuy period. Whatever was motivating him, it must have been one hell of a party at his table!

BUBBLES

Every tournament poker player is acquainted with the bubble, the line dividing the money-winners from the "also-rans." In multiday tournaments, however, there is often an artificial "bubble effect" that infects some players at the end of the first or second day. Having lasted this long, these players may unconsciously tighten up as the day winds to a close, content to merely survive into the next day of play. This kind of behavior is especially evident at the *World Series of Poker*, as no one wants to confess to their friends that they didn't make it past the first day!

I take advantage of this artificial bubble. I have often been able to add a large number of chips to my stack by playing extra tight for the first half of the day's last round of play, then switching gears to go on a complete tear through the second half. I find that many of my tired opponents, who just want to go home or off to dinner, are unwilling to risk a lot of their chips.

There is, however, a dangerous flip side to this strategy. Some players, especially if they're shortstacked, will play incredibly recklessly at the end of the day. "If I'm going to come back tomorrow," I hear them say, "I might as well have some chips."

LAST HAND BEFORE A BREAK

I will very often take a shot at stealing the blinds on the last hand before a break, regardless of my position.

Many of my opponents will fold hands that they would otherwise call me with—because they are tired, need to use the bathroom, want to run and tell their friends all about the bad beat they took during this level, etc. I've found that my steal attempts here work about twice as often as usual. If the end of the level also brings an end to the day, this strategy is even more powerful. No one wants to go broke on the last hand of the day!

I'll sometimes "help" my tired-looking opponents survive long enough to make it out the door. "Looks like we've got time for just a few more hands," I'll point out. Then, while they breathe their sighs of relief, I'll steal two or three hands in a row.

IMPLICIT COLLUSION LATE IN A TOURNAMENT

Here's an interesting situation that often arises late in a tournament: It is often good strategy to "implicitly collude" with an opponent to bust another opponent on a very short stack.

Say you're nearing the end of a supersatellite in which the top five finishers will win a seat into a bigger event. There are six players left, all of whom have plenty of chips except for the one unfortunate soul who is supershort stacked in the big blind.

In this situation everyone at the table, regardless of their hole cards, should flat call. The odds of the big blind surviving against five random hands are less than 17%.

After the flop, turn, or river, it is almost always wrong to bet, even if you've flopped a very good hand— you don't want to scare off an opponent who has a chance of eliminating the short stack.

I once found myself one of six players left in a tournament that paid the top five finishers. I got into a four-way hand with A-T, making two pair when the flop came A-T-4.

Like a dummy, I bet my hand. Everyone had to fold except the short stack, who was all-in with 7-4. A third four came on the turn, winning the pot for the short stack. As it turned out, one of the players I scared off with my bet was holding K-4 and would have won the pot, eliminating the short stack, had I just "checked it down" and allowed him to stay in.

Instead, the short-stacked player began what turned out to be a miraculous comeback that included knocking *me* out on the bubble. I was bitter but had no one to blame but myself.

I do not think that this kind of implicit collusion against a short stack represents unethical behavior. I would never say something like, "Okay, guys, let's all take a shot—no one bet or raise." I'm merely hoping that my fellow players are aware of this strategy. If it seems like they might not be, I see no problem in educating them away from the table while on a break or in between rounds.

SOBERING MATH AND BAD BEATS

While tournament poker is a pursuit that demands a lot of skill, there is no doubt in my mind that it requires an extraordinary amount of luck to win.

Over the course of a tournament, I'm due to be dealt pocket aces about 1 out of 221 hands. At typical tournament dealing speeds I pick them up about once every five hours or so.

For this thought experiment, I assume that for every 221st hand I play, I pick up A♣ A♦. I raise. Then a "sucker" at the table, who has exactly the same number of chips that I have, loves his hand and re-raises. I move all-in and he calls.

I am all-in with the best hand. A dominant best hand. He turns over K♠ K♥ and is crushed to see my aces. I am 81.26% to win before the flop.

Over the course of five days of play, ten hours a day, I face this situation ten times. Ten times I have to "not get unlucky" in order to win the tournament. What are the chances?

A-A vs. K-K All-in	Chance of Survival
1st time	81.26%
2nd	66.02%
3rd	53.65%
4th	43.59%
5th	35.42%
6th	28.78%
7th	23.39%
8th	19.00%
9th	15.44%
10th	12.55%

In other words I have only slightly better than a 50% chance to survive the first three of these confrontations! I will have taken a bad beat 46.35% of the time.

To win a major poker tournament I must survive many of these all-in confrontations. Chris "Jesus" Ferguson, the 2000 *World Series of Poker* champion, told me that a few days after he won the bracelet he went back and "did the math" on every hand where most or all of his chips were on the line. At the end of his tournament he had nearly $6,000,000 in chips. Chris calculated that, in expected value, he probably should have closer to $25,000 in front of him. In short, Chris was all-in several times in the tournament with the worst hand, and he was all-in several times in the tournament with the best hand. Bottom line is this: Being all-in gives you an opportunity to be all-out.

Bad beats are a part of the game. Anyone who thinks differently just doesn't understand the mathematics of probability. Surviving and getting to the final table is, indeed, a skillful pursuit, but there will be many, many times where chance, more than skill, will determine fate.

No Limit Hold'em is a little like Russian Roulette—one out of six chambers in the gun is loaded. I can keep pulling the trigger but eventually, well, I'll be toast.

The key to this very difficult game is to realize that the bad beats will happen. If I'm going to take a bad beat, I do my best to make sure that my opponent has fewer chips than I have. I remember this:

I cannot go broke in a poker tournament if I'm never all-in against a bigger stack.

SOME PERCENTAGES AND MATH

Yes, math does play a huge role in poker. But as far as math goes, what you need to know isn't all that complicated—it's nothing a reasonably able fourth grader couldn't handle with a little bit of practice.

The most important—and most difficult—chore is calculating pot odds and implied odds. All that is required, however, is simple addition, multiplication, and division. Higher math and statistical wizardry is rarely, if ever, necessary during the course of play.

The following chapter will help guide you through the mathematical concepts that will make you a better No

Limit Hold'em player. I have done my best to make these pages as straightforward and easy to understand as possible. If you find you are getting confused, take a deep breath, get out some chips, a pencil and some paper, and run through the examples a few times. If it gets too frustrating, feel free to jump to the next section on psychology. Over time, poker math becomes second nature and you will nearly always do the right thing.

THE RULES OF FOUR
AND TWO

———◆◆———

I have found a quick and easy way of figuring out how often I will draw to a winning hand after the flop.

First I count my "outs," or the cards that will give me a winning hand. For example, let's say I have T♣ 9♦ and I put my opponent on A-K (as it turns out, he has A♠ K♦). The flop comes A♣ T♦ 7♠. My opponent is in front, of course, having flopped a pair of aces, but there are five cards—the two remaining tens and the three nines—that will put me in front. In other words, I have five outs.

I can calculate the approximate odds of catching one of my cards on the turn or the river by multiplying the number of outs I have by four. In this case:

$$5 \times 4 = 20\%$$

According to this "Rule of Four," I have about a 20% chance of catching a winning card on the turn or the river. The actual odds turn out to be 21.2%, a tiny difference that is irrelevant for most purposes.

With only the river card to come, the "Rule of

Four" becomes the "Rule of Two." Let's say the 8♣ comes on the turn. Not one of five outs we're looking for, but it turns our hand into an open-ended straight draw that can be completed by any jack or six. The additional eight outs gives me thirteen in all. Using the Rule of Two:

$$13 \times 2 = 26\%$$

The actual percentage turns out to be 29.5%, but once again that is close enough.

For purists who insist on exactitude, I have included a table at the end of the book that lists the precise percentages. See "Outs" on page 270.

(Note: The Rule of Four breaks down slightly with a massive number of outs. With fifteen or more outs, the formula overestimates the chances of winning. But the chances of winning with that many outs are so big that it will almost never matter. Plus, you usually only have that many outs in Omaha, not in Texas Hold'em.)

A-K, A-A, K-K

There are sixteen ways to make an A-K hand:

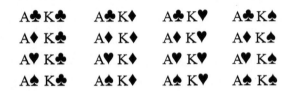

A♣ K♣	A♣ K♦	A♣ K♥	A♣ K♠
A♦ K♣	A♦ K♦	A♦ K♥	A♦ K♠
A♥ K♣	A♥ K♦	A♥ K♥	A♥ K♠
A♠ K♣	A♠ K♦	A♠ K♥	A♠ K♠

There are six ways to make an A-A hand:

| A♣ A♦ | A♣ A♥ | A♣ A♠ |
| A♦ A♥ | A♦ A♠ | A♥ A♠ |

Likewise, there are six ways to make a K-K hand:

| K♣ K♦ | K♣ K♥ | K♣ K♠ |
| K♦ K♥ | K♦ K♠ | K♥ K♠ |

So if I'm up against an opponent in a situation where he'd only raise with A-A, K-K, or A-K, the odds are sixteen to twelve that he's holding A-K.

If he'll also raise with Q-Q—another six possibilities—then it becomes more likely (eighteen to sixteen) that he's holding a pocket pair.

THE VALUE OF SUITEDNESS

Everybody knows how valuable being "suited" is, right?

Actually, no. Having two hole cards of the same suit turns out to be a far smaller advantage than most inexperienced players believe. Many new players overestimate the chances of making a flush when they are suited. Some of the celebrities on *Celebrity Poker Showdown*, when posed this question, stated that their chances of making a flush by the river when starting suited were "about 20%."

K♠ K♥ vs. 8♦ 7♦

With all the money in the pot, the suited 8-7 will win about 23% of the time.

K♠ K♥ vs. 8♦ 7♣

With all the money in the pot, the unsuited 8-7 will win about 19% of the time.

K♠ K♥ vs. A♣ 8♣

With all the money in the pot, the suited ace will win about 32% of the time.

K♠ K♥ vs. A♦ 8♣

With all the money in the pot, the unsuited ace will win about 29% of the time.

In each case, you can clearly see that suited cards will only outperform their unsuited cousins around 3–4% of the time. In other words, the main strength of a hand comes from the rank of the cards, not their suitedness. A decision whether to play or fold a hand before the flop has to be *very* close before I consider whether or not it is suited.

PREFLOP MATCHUPS

While actually calculating the preflop percentages of two competing hands gets pretty complicated, I can approximate my chances of winning by memorizing just a few scenarios.

Fav = The favorite to win the hand
Dog = The underdog in the hand
Odds = If the favorite is 82% to win, and the underdog is 18% to win, the better hand would be an 82-to-18, or 4.6-to-1 favorite. This

would mean that there would need to be $46 in the pot for each $10 I am being asked to call.

(In each situation the favorite is listed first.)

Situation	Example	Fav	Dog	Odds
Pair vs. Underpair	AA vs. 55	82	18	4.6
Pair vs. Under-suited-connectors	KK vs. 87s	77	23	3.3
Pair vs. Suited over and under	TT vs. A2s	68	32	2.1
Pair vs. Connected suited overcards	77 vs. KQs	51	49	1.0
Pair vs. Connected overcards	77 vs. KQo	54	46	1.2
Suited connectors	JT♠ vs. 65♥	63	37	1.7
High card vs. Two intermediates	A2 vs. Q8	58	42	1.4
High/low vs. Med. suited connectors	A2 vs. QJs	53	47	1.1
Domination	ATs vs. A2	70	30	2.3
Two high vs. Two low	KT vs. 64	64	36	1.8
High/low vs. Medium/lower	Q7 vs. T5	63	37	1.7
Best vs. Worst	AA vs. 72	89	11	8.1
Unsuited vs. Suited	AKs vs. AKo	53	47	1.1

AKs denotes A and K of the same suit. AKo denotes A and K of two different suits.

SLIGHT DOG, BIG FAVORITE

A-K is one of the best hands to play in No Limit Hold'em. Many top professionals play this hand very aggressively, almost as if they had A-A or K-K. Why so? Because with this hand, most of the time either they will be a very slight underdog (they are against a pocket pair) or they'll be a big favorite (against A-Q, etc.)

Computer simulation with A-K against a random selection of decent hands (any pocket pair A-A to 2-2, A-K, A-Q, A-J, K-Q) shows that A-K comes out slightly ahead, winning 53.23% of the time against all of these hands. Only against A-A is the A-K truly dominated. Even against K-K, the A-K will win about 31% of the time.

INTERESTING, UNEXPECTED MATCHUPS

Here are some preflop matchups whose results turn out to be interesting and unexpected:

Against A-J or 8-8, K-Q is an underdog. But look what happens against A-J *and* 8-8:

A♣ J♦	30.2%
K♦ Q♦	36.4%
8♠ 8♥	33.4%

K-Qs suddenly become a nice favorite!
Here is the closest preflop equity race I've been able to find:

K♣ Q♣	33.3334%
K♦ Q♦	33.3334%
8♥ 4♠	33.3332%

Ask most professional poker players which of the following hands is the favorite before the flop:

J♣ T♣ vs. 5♠ 5♥

Most will answer 5-5. I know I did. I thought that every pocket pair was favored over two unpaired cards. In this case, 5-5 seems to be in the lead, but the J-T suited turns out to be a reasonable favorite:

185

J♣ T♣	52.46%
5♠ 5♥	47.54%

POT ODDS AND IMPLIED ODDS

The most complicated math I have to perform on a regular basis involves pot odds and implied odds. Being able to calculate these odds is critical to making correct decisions at the table. I'll use examples to illustrate each concept.

——POT ODDS——

My opponent and I each have $2,500 in chips. There is already $5,000 in the pot when the turn card arrives. My opponent goes all-in, creating a $7,500 pot. Should I call?

First, I need to calculate the pot odds, or the amount of money I stand to win relative to the amount of money I'll have to put at risk. Pot odds are usually described as a ratio, or *x* to one:

Pot odds = (Total pot ÷ amount I'm asked to call) to 1

Or in this example:

$$(\$7{,}500 \div \$2{,}500) = 3 \text{ to } 1$$

So, I'm getting three to one on my $2,500 call. What the hell does that mean? Not much, until I calculate the percentage of the time I need to make a winning hand in order to justify calling the bet. What "three to one" actually means is that in order to break even I'll need to win this bet one time for every three times I lose. Here's where it gets a little tricky—three losses plus one win actually equals *four* outcomes. When calculating my break even percentage, or BEP, I have to add that extra outcome to the formula:

Break even percentage = 1 / (Pot Odds + 1)

Or in this example:

$$\text{BEP} = 1 / (3 + 1) = 1 / 4 = 25\%$$

In this case I will need to make the winning hand 25% of the time to break even. As long as I have a 25% chance or better of winning, it is correct for me to call. Less than 25%, and the mathematically proper play is to throw my hand away.

In No Limit Hold'em, facing all-in bets is a common occurrence. Mastering pot-odds calculations is necessary to become a great, winning player in these circumstances.

——IMPLIED ODDS——

In the example above I was facing an all-in bet, which gave me the luxury of knowing that the $2,500 I was asked to call was the only money that I would have to risk.

It gets more complicated when my opponent has enough chips left to do some betting after the next card is dealt. I have to resort to "Implied Odds" to figure out what to do: Implied odds = [(Total pot + The amount that I'm likely to get my opponent to call in the future, after I make a winning hand) ÷ (Amount I have to call right now + The amount I'm likely to have to call in the future)] to one.

Here's an example:

My opponent has $5,000. I have $5,000. The pot has $5,000 when the turn card arrives. My opponent bets $2,500, creating a $7,500 pot. He has $2,500 remaining.

Let's say I know that if I make a winning hand on the river, my opponent will pay me off with his last $2,500. I also know that if I miss on the river, I won't have to invest another dime into this pot. So what are the implied odds associated with the $2,500 bet I'm currently asked to call?

Implied odds = [($7,500 in the pot + $2,500 I'm going to get from them if I make my hand) ÷ ($2,500 I have to call now + $0 I'm likely to have to call in the future)] to 1

The math tells me that I'm getting four to one implied odds on my call. Do I do it? I'll know after I figure out my break even percentage:

$$BEP = 1 / (4 + 1) = 1 / 5 = 20\%$$

If I have a 20% chance of catching a winning card on the river, the implied odds tell me I should play on and call his bet.

Yes, this is a little complicated. But good news: It is the most complicated math needed to play great No Limit Hold'em.

The following table lists a number of possible bets

(in relation to the size of the pot), the odds I'm getting to call, and the break even percentage that will let me know if it's correct to call. The table works for either pot odds or implied odds.

My Opponent's Bet in Relation to the Size of the Pot	Pot Odds or Implied Odds	Chance Necessary to Break Even If Call	Min # Outs Needed to Call with 2 Cards to Come	Min # Outs Needed to Call with 1 Card to Come
1/4 of the pot	5.0-1	17%	5	9
1/2 of the pot	3.0-1	25%	7	13
3/4 of the pot	2.3-1	30%	8	15
The full pot	2.0-1	33%	9	17
Double the pot	1.5-1	40%	10	20

Studying this table allows me to deduce a few key principles underlying No Limit Hold'em:

♠ If my opponent bets the size of the pot or less and is all-in after the flop, I am getting the right pot odds to call with a straight or a flush draw.
♠ If my opponent bets at least half the pot and is all-in after the turn, I am making a mistake to call with just about any drawing hand.
♠ If possible I should plan my bets in a way that will allow

me to wager at least 1/2 the pot after the turn so that my opponent will always be making a fairly big mistake to call with a draw.

If you are a math whiz who understands the principles underlying the table above, great! If you're not, I suggest committing it to memory. These scenarios will arise time and time again.

If you want a little bit more practice with pot odds and implied odds, I've posted a few practice problems on my Web site:

www.philgordonpoker.com/littlegreenbook.html

PSYCHOLOGY

You've finished the section on math, possibly with a glazed expression of confusion or helplessness. Fear not. While math is important to winning poker, psychology is even more important to the game.

No matter how great you are at math, playing by the numbers will never lead to true success. Master the psychological components of the game, however, and you can become a winning No Limit Hold'em player.

There are many great players who have never once encountered an Excel spreadsheet or resorted to the Rule of Four. It may be a painful process, but after enough years at the table, the mathematics behind poker becomes intuitive.

The same can never be said for poker psychology. Getting inside the minds of your opponents, figuring out their weaknesses, devising plans to separate them from their chips, staying off tilt, knowing when to change gears—these concepts require constant vigilance and effort.

BIG LAYDOWNS

To win at No Limit Hold'em I must be capable of making a big laydown.

Many situations arise where I have a great hand and there is a lot of money in the pot but careful analysis suggests that my great hand might not be the best hand. Being able to avoid these traps is critical to my success. As hard as it might seem I've simply got to be able to fold.

When I'm considering making a big laydown, several factors come to mind:

♦ Is my opponent's play consistent with what I know about him? If yes, I'm more likely to lay down a big hand. If no, I'm more likely to go ahead and call.

♦ Am I really pot committed? If I am getting the right pot odds to call with cards to come, I have to do it or I'm making a mistake. Laydowns when the pot odds dictate a call are not big laydowns—they are big mistakes.

♦ Do my opponents respect my play? If they do, I am more likely to fold and make the big laydown. If not, I am more likely to call.

♦ Have I been forced off good hands recently? If yes, I'm more likely to call. I can't become a pushover at the table. If no, I'm more likely to fold.

♦ Can my opponent afford to be making a mistake in this situation? If yes, I'm more likely to call. If no, I'm more likely to fold.

The biggest laydown I've ever made took place at the 2001 *World Series of Poker* championship event. We were down to thirteen players on two tables. I was the chip leader at my table, with nearly $650,000, about $200,000 more than the average stack. The second biggest stack—about $620,000—belonged to Phil Hellmuth Jr. Play had become extremely tight, as everyone was trying to squeeze into the next day's final table, which would be televised by the Discovery Channel. We hadn't seen a flop in about an hour.

With blinds at $3,000/$6,000 and $1,000 antes, Mike Matusow—one of the best and most dangerous players in the world—opened from first position with a $20,000 raise. The next two players folded to me. I peeked at my cards and immediately began to shake: K-K. Yes, I was shaking. I'm sure of it. Doing my best to restore a sense of calm, I raised to $100,000. I didn't necessarily want to see the flop, but figured that I was pot committed if Mike re-raised all-in with his remaining $300,000 or so.

But Mike wouldn't get the chance. The action got to the small blind, where it took Phil Hellmuth Jr. less than fifteen seconds to push *his* entire stack into the middle.

Mike grimaced as he folded, showing what I thought was Q-Q to the crowd. Now it was up to me. "My God," I remember thinking, "Phil's got pocket aces."

But could I really lay down pocket kings? I tried to steady myself and took a few moments to examine the evidence:

♣ Is my opponent's play consistent with what I know about him? Yes. If Phil did indeed have A-A, he wouldn't get fancy. There was already $150,000 in the pot and he was out of position. The all-in move would certainly be the most likely way he'd play his aces.

♣ Am I really pot committed? No. If I fold, I'll still have $550,000, an above-average stack.

♣ Does my opponent respect my play? Not really. Phil Hellmuth Jr. doesn't respect anyone's play other than his own. That being said, he had to respect my raise, since the last three hands I'd shown down were pocket aces (twice) and A-K suited.

♣ Have I been forced off good hands recently? No. It had been a long while since I'd been in a confrontation.

♣ Can my opponent afford to be making a mistake in this situation? Definitely not. As I said, the last three hands I'd shown were powerhouses. I had just re-raised an under the gun raiser. Phil had to seriously consider the possibility that I had A-A. Phil would not risk his entire tournament if he thought I could have him completely dominated.

The evidence seemed to support my initial instinct: Phil had to have A-A. I threw my kings into the muck.

Another player might have been content to let me stew over my decision, but not Phil Hellmuth Jr. He proudly flipped over his aces. "What'd you have, Gordon," he jabbed. "Ace-queen?"

"Nope," I replied. "Just kings." Unable to believe I was capable of making this kind of laydown, Phil challenged me. I pulled my kings out of the muck and showed them to a cheering crowd. It was one of those defining moments that life will occasionally send your way—not only had I made the best laydown of my life, but I had earned the respect of the room. I went on to finish the tournament in fourth place—one spot better than Phil Hellmuth Jr.

BURY THEM

"I look into their eyes, shake their hand, pat
their back, and wish them luck, but I am
thinking, 'I am going to bury you.'"
—Seve Ballesteros, Masters champion

I do my best to be a likeable guy at the poker table. Pleasant. Courteous. Affable.

But please don't mistake my good nature for anything resembling sympathy. Once the cards are in the air, my primary goal is to bust each and every one of my opponents.

I will never softplay anyone, not even a friend, and I would not respect a friend who played softly against me. Whatever relationships that exist in the outside world are forgotten at the table. No allegiances, no friendship, no mercy. It's every man and woman for themselves.

Speaking of which, some men, whether hindered by physical attraction or unconscious sexism, seem to play softer against the ladies. Not me. I play equally hard against both sexes. May the best player win.

AFTER A BAD BEAT

When I take a bad beat, I try to shake it off as quickly as I can. I'll often just pretend that I've doubled up after making a great play, or that it was *me* who just got lucky against another unfortunate soul. My stack is still going to be my stack. All I can control is my outlook.

One interesting aspect to a bad beat is the psychological impact it will have on my opponents. They may not know that I've already moved on. They might even think that I'm on tilt. I've found that my opponents will very often play looser and more aggressively against me after I've taken a bad beat.

A perfect example occurred at the 2001 *World Series of Poker*. We were down to about fifty-five players. I picked up pocket aces in late position, made my standard raise, then quickly called the big blind when he re-raised me all-in. He was in awful shape after turning over his pocket nines, but a third nine on the flop cost me the pot and about half my stack.

I was devastated, of course, but didn't go on tilt. "Nice hand, sir," I told him, then went about pretending that it was me who had just doubled up.

I thought I was still in the land of make-believe when I looked at the very next hand I was dealt: pocket aces again! I made the very same preflop raise. The player on the button, assuming that I was still steaming from the earlier beat, came over the top of me with a re-raise. I decided to just call, intending to trap him on the flop.

The flop cooperated—a T-7-2 rainbow—and when I checked to my opponent, he bet all-in. I was more than happy to call. His incorrect assessment of my psychological state had led him to make this play without a pair or even a draw. I regained a lot of the chips I'd just lost.

SUPERSTITIONS

"It's bad luck to be superstitious."
—Andrew Mathis

RUSHES

Many players believe in "rushes," those seemingly supernatural strings of hands where everything goes right. Not even great players are immune—some of the very best will almost always see the next flop after winning a big pot, just to see if they're on a rush.

There is no such thing as a rush—not mathematically, anyway. From a psychological perspective, however, it's a completely different story. An opponent who believes that I am on a rush will likely play much more carefully against me. If I loosen up my game against a player too scared or superstitious to play optimal poker, well, it won't take too long for that "rush" to become a self-fulfilling prophecy.

I'll also do my best to get involved in pots with players who believe that they are in the midst of a rush. Since they just *know* that they're going to make their hand, they will often overvalue their cards. When I flop a good hand against these kinds of players, I will overbet the pot and make them pay for their superstitious behavior.

WATCH FOR BETTING PATTERNS

I am always studying my opponents at the table, searching for betting patterns that can be exploited. Here are a few of the more common ones, and my favorite strategies for taking advantage of them:

♥ Some players always bet when they have a great hand and check when they don't. When they bet, I'm careful about continuing on, but when they check, I'll nearly always bet.

♥ Some players always bet their flush and straight draws. When the board is "flushing" or "straightening" after the flop, I am very apt to make a big raise against these players.

♥ Some players always lead at the pot with a continuation bet if they've raised before the flop. Against these players I'll often smooth-call from position with a great hand and try to trap them on the flop.

♥ Some players will bluff after the flop with just about anything, but they are incapable of following it up with a bluff on the turn. They are armed, as we say, with a one-bullet gun. Against these opponents I'll often just call their bet on the flop. If they bet after the turn, I know I'm beat. If they check, I know the pot is mine for the taking.

♥ Some players overbet when they are bluffing. When one of these players overbets the pot after the river card, I'm more likely to call.

♥ Some players under-bet the pot with weak hands. They are scared of committing chips to the pot. When they make a small bet, I raise.

Note that a single hand does not define a betting pattern. I want to see an opponent play the same type of hand the same way three or four times in a row before I decide that there's a betting pattern ready to be exploited.

I also look for betting patterns in my own game, and look to change the way that I play if it seems like my behavior is becoming routine. For example, if I've bet out my last three flush draws or straight draws, I'll check the next time I pick one up.

BEATING TIGHT AND PASSIVE PLAYERS

On the surface it would seem difficult to make much money against tight-passive players: your opponents who don't see too many flops and generally won't commit too many chips to the pot unless they've made a fantastic hand.

These players, however, have an Achilles' heel in that they fold too much. Against a tight-passive player, I find it's correct to play loose. They will fold when I bet my marginal hands or bluffs. When they finally decide to put their money in, I can quit the hand and feel confident I'm doing the right thing.

Keep in mind that in Hold'em it is very difficult to flop a great hand. A player who waits all day for A-K is only going to flop a pair or better about 35% of the time.

So while I'm unlikely to beat tight-passive players out of big pots, I am perfectly satisfied to pick up the many small pots and blinds they concede to me.

BEATING LOOSE PLAYERS

The big mistake that loose players make is putting too much money in the pot without a premium hand. To beat these players, I find it's correct to play tight. It is very difficult to flop a great hand. A player who gets involved in ten straight pots is only going to flop a pair or better 35% of the time. The other 65% of the time he'll be out of line.

Since I know the loose player can't possibly have a great hand every time he bets, I just have to wait until I have a great hand that connects with the flop. From there it's easy to bet or raise and take the pot.

BEATING CALLING STATIONS

There are some players who will literally play almost any two cards, will rarely raise, and are willing to call all the way to the river to see if they can make a hand. We call them "calling stations." I love calling stations. They make me want to ask them for their addresses so I can send them gifts the following day . . . gifts that I will buy with their money.

The calling station is far and away the most profitable opponent to play against. I will never bluff or slowplay against a calling station. I just make value bet after value bet, overbetting the pot when I have the nuts or a great hand.

BEATING OVERLY
AGGRESSIVE OPPONENTS

I am not normally a fan of slowplaying. Against overly aggressive opponents, however, I am willing to change my tune. Truly hyperaggressive players will fire two, even three bluffs at a pot when they just can't win. I am more than happy to check and call and let them bust themselves.

I realize that these players will almost always bet if I am out of position and I check the flop. I realize that these players will very often make a big bluff on the river. In fact, the scariest thing an overly aggressive player can do is make a small bet. It's usually a sign that they actually have a hand this time and they are desperate to get paid off.

Against my overly aggressive opponents, I am willing to give up small pots in the hopes of getting paid off in a big way when I have a great hand.

Playing overly aggressive poker against an overly aggressive opponent will often turn a poker game into a crapshoot. I made the mistake of playing an overly aggressive style against Juha Helppi, the Finnish "amateur" who beat the living daylights out of me in the first season of the *World Poker Tour*. I should have let him bust himself instead of continually applying pressure on him with substandard hands. Lesson learned—on national television no less!

WHEN TO CHANGE GEARS

Late in the third day of the 2001 *World Series of Poker* championship event, I found myself seated at a very tight table. There were forty-seven players left in the tournament, forty-five of whom would make the money. I began to do what I often like to do on the bubble: steal blinds. I played nearly every pot, raising two-and-a-half times the big blind each time, successfully stealing nearly $100,000 in blinds and antes. Finally, someone raised me back. "Okay," I thought, "maybe he picked up aces." Next hand, I was back in with a raise. This time a different player re-raised me. Now I knew it was personal. The table had taken just about enough from me, realizing that I couldn't have a hand every time. It was time for me to change gears.

I change gears when I believe the dynamics and conditions at the table have shifted enough to warrant a change in strategy.

I gear up, or play more aggressively:

- ♠ when an opponent busts out, especially at the final table
- ♠ when the blinds have just been increased
- ♠ if my opponents are scared of me or if I have a tight image
- ♠ if my opponent just got caught bluffing

I gear down, or play more conservatively:

- ♦ when there has been a significant change in my stack, positive or negative
- ♦ when a big hand has just taken place at the table—people will need some time to figure out how the table dynamics have changed
- ♦ when I arrive at a new table
- ♦ when there are many short stacks
- ♦ if I was particularly active in the previous round
- ♦ if I've been caught bluffing recently
- ♦ if someone at the table believes they are "on a rush"

SEAT SELECTION

Seat selection can be one of the most important factors in winning at No Limit Hold'em. When I have the option of choosing my own seat, I like to position loose, weak players on my right and the tight players on my left.

By keeping the loose players on my right, I'll be able to raise and isolate them. I'll also have superior position before and after the flop.

With tight players on my left I'll be able to steal their blinds when I'm on the button.

FORMING A GAME PLAN

I try to form an individual game plan for beating each and every opponent at the table. Here are some of the weaknesses I've spotted frequently, and the methodology I use to exploit each one.

♣ **Players who habitually overbet the pot after the flop**
I will try to play a lot of hands against these players, from position. I am willing to take the worst of it

before the flop for the chance of getting the very best of it after the flop. I might even resort to "limping" in order to get into more pots with them postflop.

♣ **Players who habitually underbet the pot after the flop**

Drawing hands generally have little value in No Limit Hold'em when players are betting correctly. Against players who underbet the flop, however, I will play more drawing hands, even from out of position, as I'll be getting the right price to chase my draws.

♣ **Players who frequently check-raise**

Against these players I will almost always bet a strong hand and almost always check a drawing hand.

♣ **Players who will call oversize bets with only a draw**

I will usually bet the size of the pot—sometimes more, but never less.

♣ **Players who habitually slowplay big hands**

I tend to check when they check, and raise if they bet.

♣ **Players who rarely defend their blinds**

I will raise often and liberally when they are in the blinds.

♣ **Players who defend their blinds too much**

I will generally wait for a premium hand to raise, and will overbet the pot when I do—maybe five to six times the big blind instead of the usual three to four.

SHOWING MY CARDS

I almost never show my cards after a hand. I realize that each and every time I show a hand that I do not have to reveal, I am giving my opponents information they can use against me later. Showing a big bluff or a big laydown is definitely a big ego boost. But it is a short-lived buzz with detrimental results. It affects my ability to make future bluffs, or it encourages my opponents to play more aggressively against me.

If I choose to show a hand or two in a tournament, I will always note the situation, how I played it, and who was paying attention. The next time I have a similar hand in a similar situation, I will go out of my way to play it in a different manner.

TILT

Shake a pinball machine too hard, and it will "tilt." The same can be said for a poker player who gets shaken at the table. Players go on tilt for all kinds of reasons:

- ♥ They receive a bad beat.
- ♥ They make a bad play.
- ♥ The tournament director makes a ruling that doesn't suit them.
- ♥ The cocktail waitress or chip runner is slow to attend to their needs.
- ♥ They are being lectured or needled by another player at the table.
- ♥ Their significant other calls and asks them to quit the game and come home.
- ♥ They have been subject to a long streak of unplayable hands.
- ♥ They have missed the flop many times in a row.
- ♥ A bad player at the table is getting very lucky and winning many pots.
- ♥ A bad player is getting manhandled by a good player while the tilter is forced to wait for an opportunity that never seems to come.
- ♥ They were just told to change tables, and they moved into a blind that represents a significant portion of their stack.

Most players who are on tilt will play more aggressively. They will call very big bets without the best hand. They will take more chances. And they will target the person who sent them on tilt.

However, other tilters will play a very loose, passive game. They will limp into nearly every pot and call every raise out of position, hoping to get even by flopping a monster.

Here are some of the symptoms that help me identify players who have gone on tilt:

♠ They mutter under their breath.
♠ They shake their heads in disbelief.
♠ They are visibly angry with a player at the table.
♠ They berate the dealer or floorman.
♠ They give "lessons" to players who just beat them.
♠ They call too many raises with subpremium hands, in order to catch up or deliver a compensating bad beat.

When I identify a player on tilt, I will look for an opportunity to take advantage of their emotional state. I might even work on keeping them on tilt . . . just a little.

IMPLIED TILT ODDS

Some players can get so thrown out of whack by a bad beat or a bad play that their games will fall apart. The most extreme cases will "tilt off" all their money with mistimed aggression and incredibly bad decision-making.

If I know a guy is capable of imploding after a bad beat, I'll go out of my way to deliver one. Yes, I know that I am bucking the odds. But I'm occasionally willing to take the worst of it against a potential tilter, because if I get lucky, my poor opponent will throw money at me for the next fifty hands. My "implied tilt odds" are very big.

This is much more relevant to cash games than tournaments, however. Tournament players nearly always go broke before I can take full advantage of any implied tilt odds that I manage to attract by giving a bad beat.

GAME SELECTION

If I have a choice of ring games, I will look for the one that best suits my strengths and mood. If I am in a gambling mood, I will look for a tight table. Tight tables will, in the long run, be more profitable for me because I'll be able to steal their blinds and pots more effectively.

If I am in a grinding mood, I will look for a loose table. If I know that I don't have my A-game, I prefer to sit at a loose table and play very tight. This is almost always a winning strategy.

If I am on tilt or steaming, I will look for a brown table—the kitchen table at home.

TIMING OF BETS

I try to always take about the same amount of time to consider my options and take action on a hand. Not too fast, not too slow.

I will occasionally be faced with a difficult decision that requires me to think a little longer. I'll take the time I need, of course, but will be acutely aware that my departure from the norm has provided my opponent with information about the strength of my hand.

BLUFFING

If I never get bluffed out of a pot, I know I am calling too much. Conversely, if I never get caught bluffing, I know I'm not bluffing enough.

Early in a particular tournament or session I will often test an opponent by making a bluff. An opponent who will call a reasonable pot-size bet with a marginal holding is not likely to be "bluffable" in the future.

MAKING THE BIG BLUFF

There are bluffs, and there are BIG bluffs.

The little bluffs—stealing blinds, antes, and small pots with well-timed bets—are just a part of the game. The big bluff is a work of art. Before I'll consider risking a huge portion of my stack on a hand I'm almost certain is second-best, I'll run through the following checklist in my head:

♦ My opponent believes I am playing tight.
♦ My opponent has not recently witnessed a bluff from me.

♦ My opponent has not recently been the target of a big bluff from another player. Players who have been bluffed off a hand (and had their noses rubbed in it) or have caught another player bluffing are more apt to call.

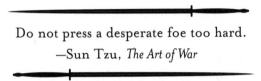

Do not press a desperate foe too hard.
—Sun Tzu, *The Art of War*

♦ My opponent is very likely on a weak or medium-strength hand.
♦ The tournament situation makes it very hard for my opponent to call: We're on the bubble, he has a big stack and can only get busted by me, or we're in the money and there are many short stacks that will likely go broke soon.
♦ The pot is very large.
♦ I am very sure that my hand is losing and cannot win without a bet.
♦ My opponent is unlikely to have a very good draw.
♦ My opponent isn't anywhere near pot committed.
♦ My bet will severely cripple my opponent's stack if he calls and I actually have the hand I'm representing.
♦ I have represented strength throughout the hand, or it

is very plausible in the context of the betting that I have been helped enormously by the last card dealt.

The biggest bluff I've ever made in a tournament took place at the 2004 Bay 101 Shooting Star tournament in San Jose. It was down to the final four players, and I held a slight chip lead over Masoud Shojaei, $800,000 to $600,000.

I had been playing pretty tight (for a four-handed game, that is) and had not shown down a bluff in the preceding few hours. I felt that I had the respect of the table.

With the blinds at $5,000/$10,000 with $2,000 antes, Masoud raised to $35,000 from under the gun. I didn't have a great hand, K-3 offsuit, but I sensed that he was weak. Trusting my instincts, I raised to $135,000 from the small blind, hoping to take the pot right there.

Masoud called quickly. I nearly threw up. "Phil," I said to myself, "you are done with this hand. You are not going to put another chip in this pot unless you flop the nuts. Period."

The flop came 9♣ 8♦ 6♠ and I checked. Then a funny thing happened—Masoud checked behind me. My eyes lit up. Masoud never slowplays, especially when the pot is as big as this one was. He would have bet just about any reasonable hand there. I'm almost sure he would have bet any hand A-T or better. He must have been weak. I put him on K-Q, K-J, K-T, or a small pocket pair.

The turn came a Q♣. This looked like a "good card" for my hand. Unless he had K-Q, Masoud was unlikely to have improved his hand. A bet here would certainly get him to fold a hand like K-J or a small pocket pair. Gathering my courage, I pushed $200,000 into the middle.

I nearly wet myself when Masoud called. The crowd gasped. What could he have?

I knew for certain that if he'd had K-Q, he would have moved all-in. I didn't think he would call with a small pocket pair unless it was 8-8, and I think he would have bet that hand on the flop. It just didn't add up. And then I saw it: K-T of clubs would definitely warrant a call. He'd have a flush draw, and a double gut-shot straight draw. He *thought* he was on a draw. Little did he know that he not only had the best hand but he had me drawing nearly dead.

The river was the queen of diamonds. I quickly ran through my mental checklist:

♣ My opponent believes I am playing tight. TRUE ENOUGH

♣ My opponent has not recently witnessed a bluff from me. TRUE

♣ My opponent has not recently been the target of a big bluff from another player. TRUE

♣ My opponent is very likely on a weak or medium-strength hand. TRUE

♣ The tournament situation makes it very hard for my opponent to call. TRUE (If he's wrong, it will cost him $100,000 in real cash.)

♣ The pot is very large. VERY, VERY TRUE

♣ I am very sure that my hand is losing and cannot win without a bet. VERY TRUE

♣ My opponent is unlikely to have a very good draw. NOT ANYMORE, THE RIVER HAS BEEN DEALT

♣ My opponent isn't anywhere near pot committed. IF HE FOLDS, HE'LL BE IN THIRD CHIP POSITION WITH $250,000.

♣ My bet will severely cripple my opponent's stack if he calls and I actually have the hand I'm representing. HE'LL BE OUT IN FOURTH PLACE IF HE'S WRONG.

♣ I have represented strength throughout the hand, or it is very plausible in the context of the betting that I have been helped enormously by the last card dealt. I RE-RAISED BEFORE THE FLOP, A VERY STRONG PLAY. I CHECKED ON THE FLOP, BUT I COULD HAVE BEEN GOING FOR A CHECK-RAISE. I BET THE TURN VERY STRONGLY. I HAVE REPRE-

SENTED A HAND LIKE K-Q OR A-Q WITH MY
ACTIONS THUS FAR IN THIS HAND.

The stage was set. All I had to do was muster the
courage to pull it off. Taking a deep breath, I pushed all-in.

Masoud folded instantly. In my excitement I
exposed my bluff and instantly regretted doing so. I do
not like to show up my opponents at the table. I apolo-
gized to Masoud after the tournament was over. Later,
while watching the television broadcast, I found out
Masoud was indeed holding the K♣T♣.

MISCELLANEOUS

There are many factors that contribute to a winning player's success. Not all of them involve pot odds, psychology, or even poker itself. In this section I outline some of the miscellaneous factors that can lead to a higher win rate and a bigger bankroll.

STAKES AND BANKROLL

I know I am playing in a game that is too big for me when I know I have the best hand (but not the nuts) and I am not willing to put all the money into the pot.

Playing within my bankroll is vital to my chances of success at No Limit Hold'em. I consider a buy-in for a No Limit Hold'em game to be about 100 big blinds. In a game with $5/$10 blinds, I would buy in for $1,000. I believe that I need fifteen to twenty buy-ins in my total bankroll to be safe.

That being said, when a game has an unlimited buy-in, I generally like to be the guy with the most money at the table. Having the most money allows me to push even my deepest-stacked opponent into making the biggest mistake possible. At the very least I will try to buy enough chips to cover every one of the players that I can outplay. If my stack gets depleted, I will reload to cover those bad players.

I very rarely sit in a game with less than the maximum buy-in. If I believe I'm one of the best players at the table, there are plenty of reasons to get as much money on the table as possible. If not, there are plenty of reasons to find another game.

SESSION LENGTH

When I am winning and my opponents are losing, I will make every effort to stay at the table for as long as possible. I stay and play because:

♥ My opponents are chasing their losses and will be pressing.
♥ My opponents are very likely not playing their best games.
♥ My opponents are not playing optimally because they are worried about their bankrolls.

Professional player Ted Forrest may be the best in the world at long sessions. It is rumored that he once sat and played (while winning) for a 120-hour session. Needless to say, this is not a recommended practice.

If I am losing, I'll make just about any excuse to leave the table. *I'll leave even if I know I'm playing well but I have had the best of it.* I get up and leave because:

♠ My opponents are very likely playing their A-games.
♠ My opponents are not likely to give my game the respect it normally deserves.

♠ My opponents are playing with confidence.

♠ My bluffs are less likely to work because of my weak, tilting image.

STOP-LOSS OR WIN GOALS

I never place an artificial cap on wins or losses at the table—in either tournaments or cash games. My goal is to try to maximize every single hand. Many players, however, will set other kinds of goals for themselves:

♦ "I just want to be average at the end of the day."

♦ "I just want to survive to the end of this level."

♦ "I just want to make it into the money."

♦ "I just don't want to lose $2,000 today."

♦ "I'm above average and don't have to play any more hands today."

♦ "I'm getting up from the table because I've reached my goal of winning $5,000 today."

Players that form these artificial goals play suboptimal poker. When they are below their goal, they press too hard. When they are above their goal, they relax too much.

ADVANCE SCOUTING

If I just get to a game and have no idea how the players are playing, I will do my best to observe the table for about thirty minutes before I take a seat.

If observation is impossible—maybe because I just got a table change or there was a redraw in a tournament—then I'll ask some of my poker friends if they know anything about the styles and tendencies of the players I'm up against. Information is power.

CHOPPING THE BLINDS

Chopping the blinds is a fairly common practice in cash games. When everyone folds to them, the small and big blinds can mutually agree to take back their blind bets and move to the next hand.

Why do people chop?

♣ Because they don't want to play heads-up
♣ Because the pot is very likely going to be small
♣ Because they are friends

♣ To avoid having the hand "raked" by the house
♣ To speed up the game

I never chop the blinds unless I can somehow arrange to chop when I'm the small blind (out of position) but not chop when I'm the big blind (in position). Unfortunately, there aren't too many opponents who will let me get away with that!

DON'T TAP ON THE AQUARIUM

A few years after I started playing Hold'em, I found myself at a small casino in northern California with my dear friend and fellow Tiltboy, Dave "Diceboy" Lambert.* We were having a great time killing a $10/$20 limit game.

There was one particularly bad player at the table, and Dave was getting the best of him on almost every single hand. This "fish" was the type of player who would

---

*The Tiltboys are the group of thirteen poker players from Northern California with whom I've been playing cards since 1992. Visit www.tiltboys.com for some hilarious "Trip Reports" from our early days togther.

see every single flop, chase every single draw, and pay off every single winner. He was the ultimate ATM.

After about an hour the guy started complaining about losing so much. "Well, if you didn't see every flop, you wouldn't lose every hand," responded Dave. "Man, I'm beating you like a redheaded stepchild." Needless to say, the fish got angry. I got scared—not that he'd hit Dave but that he'd change tables or leave the casino altogether. "Hey, Diceboy," I said deadpan, "please don't tap on the aquarium."

Dave laughed and immediately stopped needling the fish. Actually, he turned the entire situation around and became quite friendly with the guy, who decided to hang out with us for another three hours, long enough for two more trips to the cash machine and a $100 loan from his buddy.

Yes, this story has a moral: When there are fish in the tank, don't tap on the aquarium.

PRACTICE MAKES PERFECT

"I am a strong believer in luck and I find the harder I work the more I have of it."
—Benjamin Franklin

Nearly every great poker player was, at one time, easy money. Greatness only comes with experience and constant self-evaluation.

When I'm at the table, I am constantly looking to improve, comparing each situation with the situations that I've been in before.

SICK GAMBLERS

While most people can enjoy a healthy relationship with poker, whether as pastime or profession, there are plenty of sick gamblers out there. We're talking people with real emotional and psychological problems.

Most of these sick gamblers are soothed by losing. It's the only way that they can confirm just how unlucky, undeserving, and cursed they are. After a game I might try to help a sick gambler. But not while we're playing. It's all business at the poker table. I do not softplay anybody.

I run into sick gamblers all the time in cash games and occasionally in tournaments. They expect to get beaten. They expect the river card to help my hand. They expect that every time I'm on a draw I will get there. Against sick gamblers I will very often bet or raise when a scare card comes on the river, even if it didn't help my hand. While I might feel sorry for them, it is my duty to fulfill their expectations.

They are going to lose their money, at this table, another table, or the craps table. Someone will end up with the chips. That someone should be me.

SUNGLASSES AT THE TABLE

I do not usually wear sunglasses at the table. Nor am I a fan of players who do. Most people think that players wear sunglasses in order to hide their eyes and protect themselves from giving away tells. But I have yet to see a reliable tell linked to a player's eyes or pupil contractions.

If there's even a slight advantage to wearing sunglasses at the table, it's that they're useful for hiding the fact that a player is actually observing another player.

I definitely suggest forgoing the sunglasses when playing online poker. Wearing sunglasses in that environment will scare loved ones.

STAKING AND GETTING STAKED

Staking players in tournaments or ring games is not a winning business. I very rarely, if ever, lend money to fellow poker players.

I've been asked on many occasions if I'd like to be staked. I've never taken anyone up on it, but I would definitely consider it if I could negotiate a good deal.

I consider my average return on a $10,000 buy-in tournament to be somewhere around $30,000. That is, for every $10,000 invested I expect over the long run to make $20,000. When I've asked serious professional players what their average returns are, I've heard answers that range everywhere from $12,000 to $70,000. I think the truth lies somewhere in the middle.

I would allow someone to "buy me out" of my poker investment if in return for putting up my entry fees, this investor would allow me to keep 60% of my winnings. If I'm right about my expectation, that investor could expect to win $2,000 every time they staked me for a tournament. If you're out there, I'm ready to sign on the bottom line tomorrow in gold ink!

AGGRESSION IS THE GREAT EQUALIZER

When I find myself playing shorthanded against a better player, I remind myself that aggression is the great equalizer. It is very difficult—in fact mathematically impossible—for a player to beat a hyperaggressive opponent more than about two thirds of the time if each player starts with twenty-five big blinds or fewer.

A classic example of this hyperaggressive approach was on display when Dewey Tomko began heads-up play against Paul "Dot Com" Phillips during the second season of the *World Poker Tour*. Suffering a four to one chip disadvantage, Dewey decided to move all-in on nearly every hand. This put Paul in quite a fix. When do you call a guy that moves in on every hand?

Say I'm playing heads-up at the end of a tournament with the world's greatest player. We both have twenty-five big blinds. If I move in on every single hand, even if my opponent knows what I'm doing, they can't beat me more than 65% of the time. Do they call me when they pick up A-7? If they do, and they're up against 7-2 (my worst holding), they'll be a 75%-25% favorite. If they're up against a hand like 8-3, they'll be a 65%-35% favorite.

Against a small pocket pair they'll be a 45%-55% under-dog. Against A-8 or better they'll be 75%-25% to lose. The point is this: They'd probably have to call with A-7, knowing that I was moving in on every hand, but they'll never be more than about 60% against two random cards.

Being hyperaggressive against the best players in the world is almost always a better strategy than playing a tight-passive game. I will not let myself get chipped away and blinded out.

TOURNAMENT STRUCTURES

The best tournaments—the ones that favor skill over luck—are the ones with the longer levels and the more gradual increases in the blinds. I believe the structure of the *World Series of Poker* is the absolute best, at least as far as my game is concerned.

In contrast, very fast tournament structures require a few changes in strategy:

♥ Because the blinds are going up rapidly, I am forced to play "faster"—more hands and a lot more aggression.

♥ I must take fifty-fifty chances earlier in the tournament

than I would with a slow structure. I hope to get lucky and be in a commanding chip position early. I'll need those chips to outlast the fast increases in the blinds during the tournament's middle stages.

♥ I expect that most of my opponents will play too tight for the structure.

♥ Each and every chip committed to the pot must be done with a real purpose.

♥ I am much more likely to employ the all-in bet to protect my hand whenever the pot has any kind of significant money in it. In fact, I am often reduced to simply going all-in or folding before the flop. After the flop, slowplaying is almost completely removed from my repertoire.

I've included the *WSOP* tournament structure and the tournament structure from FullTiltPoker.com's single table Sit & Go in the "Charts and Tables" chapter. See page 260.

ONLINE POKER

One of the biggest factors in poker's recent explosion is the growth of online poker. At any time of day or night I can log on to FullTiltPoker.com and find a game at just about any stake. The games are fast and friendly. Best of all, they're full of fish. It is easy money.

I love playing online because it is so fast. I can play four games at a time, playing seventy to one hundred hands per hour at each table. In a single hour of online play, I'll play two hundred fifty to four hundred hands! Compare that to the measly thirty to forty hands an hour at a casino, and it is easy to see why playing online is so attractive to an action junkie like me.

But playing online does require some adjustments to my game:

♠ I play a much more straightforward game. Because most of my opponents are novices or inexperienced, the more advanced plays will not work against them. Subtlety is lost on inexperienced players.

♠ I play much tighter than I do in a casino. Online poker is full of loose players. I have to tighten up to be playing properly, especially in the early stages of a tournament. Playing multiple tables at the same time necessitates playing tighter as well because my attention will be blurred between tables and situations.

♠ There are very few online tells. I have to rely more on betting patterns to smell out weakness and exploit it.

♠ My opponents, because of their inexperience, will slowplay more often than professional players. When they check to me and I have a good draw, I will very often just check and hope to catch it on the turn card.

♠ My online opponents have a hard time laying down top pair. I am very apt to overbet the pot when I flop a great hand because I know I'll get paid off if they have top pair.

♠ The Bet Pot button and the Min Raise button are frequently abused and misused. I take a little bit of extra time to make the correct bet. Automatically using the Bet Pot button is a mistake that costs online players money. Betting half the pot or another amount is often better, though it takes more effort.

Along with some of the best professionals in the world, I play online exclusively at:

www.FullTiltPoker.com

Please come join me and the other pros of Team Full Tilt Poker for the best experience in Internet poker. Watch us play, play against us, ask your questions in real time, and *learn from the pros*.

Team Full Tilt:
Phil Gordon, Howard Lederer, Chris Ferguson, Phil Ivey, John Juanda, Erik Seidel, Erick Lindgren, Andy Bloch, Clonie Gowen, Jennifer Harman, and many more.

Pick a professional poker player, like Howard, say, and watch him play for an hour or two. Write down all of the hands that he shows down. Watch him and try to put him on hands. It will almost definitely improve your game.

PLAYER PROFILES

As I have said many times, there is more than one way to win. Many of my fellow professional poker players employ styles very different from mine and still end up at the final table.

Here are a few players I know who have enjoyed a lot of success playing in a very different way from what you've read in this book.

GUS HANSEN

Gus is one of the most aggressive players I've ever seen at the table. He pays very little attention to position. At times he seems to be playing just about any two cards. Yet there is a definite method to his "madness."

Gus wins because his opponents invariably become frustrated by his tactics and commit too many chips to the pot, trying to get him off what just has to be another trash hand. But even Gus can look down and find pocket aces or kings, and when he does, carnage ensues.

After the flop Gus is a master at sensing weakness and pouncing on it. He is not afraid to commit his entire stack with only a pair or a draw, which forces his opponents to make life or death decisions.

Gus is also excellent at extracting maximum value from his hands. When he flops two pair against an opponent who has flopped a pair, Gus will bet and raise as much as he thinks he can milk from his opponent.

That being said, Gus is actually quite cautious after the turn or river. He may be a gambler before the flop, but he is truly a postflop specialist.

In the 2004 *Poker Superstars Invitational Tournament*, Gus was up against the very best in the game: Ivey, Brunson,

Chan, Lederer, Cloutier, Reese, and Greenstein. He was chip leader with about $1,000,000 in chips, followed by Doyle Brunson with $650,000, and the blinds were relatively small for the stack sizes. On one key hand, Gus found pocket aces and raised $30,000 before the flop. Doyle, who had a big hand himself, elected to "trap" Gus from the small blind with Q-Q by just calling the bet. Why was Doyle looking to trap Gus? Because on the previous hand Gus had made the same exact raise and shown down J♣ 4♣.

On this hand the flop came T-8-4, and Doyle checked to Gus, Gus bet $40,000, and Doyle check-raised all-in—*again a tremendous overbet of the pot.* Gus called and won. His previous loose play had frustrated Doyle into paying the ultimate price: all his chips. I am certain that against a tighter, more conservative player, Doyle would not have made this mistake.

Gus's game plan: play many, many hands. Keep the pressure on his opponents. Trade preflop expectation for huge implied odds after the flop and for the occasional mistake an opponent will make when he has a really big hand before the flop.

Because Gus is known as one of the best players in the world, many opponents go out of their way to stay out of his pots. They fold more often than they should in an effort to wait for the nuts or a great starting hand.

Gus steals them blind and then uses their own money to take a shot at busting them.

DAN HARRINGTON

Action Dan's nickname is one of the few examples of irony you will find at a poker table. He is one of the tightest players in the game, with a reputation for being the ultimate rock.

Dan's game is all about survival. He is excellent at playing with a short stack. He waits very patiently for good starting hands.

Because of his ultratight image, however, Dan can usually get away with stealing blinds as a tournament progresses. He will use those steals to stay even with the field, and then use his great hands to take the bigger pots. Dan's style is particularly well suited to tournaments that have very slow levels (ninety minutes or more) and slow blind structures.

Dan is, more than anything else, a preflop specialist. He rarely bluffs, but when he does, it almost always works. He is also a dead-money expert: When there is money in the pot that is looking for someone to step up and claim it, Dan is there to scoop it up.

Dan will almost never go broke with one pair, which is the fatal flaw of so many No Limit players.

PHIL HELLMUTH JR.

Phil wins a lot of chips because of his obnoxious personality at the table. He uses banter and chatter to control the table and action, making his opponents want to beat him so badly that they overcommit to the pot.

Phil "chops" at a lot of pots, making small "feeler" bets and raises before and after the flop to get information about the strength of his opponents' hands. He has adopted this strategy because he feels that he plays much better than they do after the flop. He's right.

Phil will lay down almost all draws and hands with only one pair if put to the test with a big raise. He looks to survive. He plays a lot of hands, but he is so good at reading his opponents and betting after the flop that he can give up a small amount of preflop expectation. His style of play, however, can lead to very large swings in the size of his stack.

Because of Phil's reputation, some people go out of their way to stay out of his, while others are hell-bent on confronting him. Against those who choose to steer clear, Phil robs them blind and uses their chips to make "great" laydowns in the middle stages of a tournament. Against those who choose to come after him, he waits for a great hand to bust them.

Phil rarely gives his opponents credit for being good players.

CHRIS "JESUS" FERGUSON

The ultimate poker theoretician, Chris Ferguson virtually never makes the wrong "math" play. If the pot odds are there, Chris is there. If they aren't, he's out of the hand.

Chris is willing to "gamble" with pocket pairs against A-K. Whereas players like Hellmuth despise the "coin flip," Chris rightly points out that the odds are more like 55%-45% in favor of the pair. He's willing to take that chance, even early in a tournament, because mathematics dictates that it's the right thing to do.

Chris plays an excellent all-around game, but he relies on tells less often than other experts. He will use them, of course, but rarely will a tell override the mathematical considerations of a given hand.

Chris doesn't believe in making many strategy

adjustments in tournaments. He has told me on many occasions, "Phil, just play your best cash game and you'll have the best chance to win the tournament. Players tend to overanalyze and overemphasize strategy adjustments in a tournament."

Chris believes, and bases most of his decisions on, the notion that his opponents are skilled, rational players.

HOWARD LEDERER

Howard is also one of the most focused individuals I have ever witnessed at the table. He concentrates on every single hand throughout the tournament or ring game, whether he is involved or not. He plays tells far more often than most of his fellow professionals, placing great faith in his ability to read his opponents. The fact that he is able to play with total fearlessness certainly doesn't hurt.

Howard is great at picking the easy money off the table. He is constantly scooping pots that are looking for an owner.

Howard plays an average number of hands. He plays very well both before and after the flop and is not afraid to make a big laydown or a big call.

JOHN JUANDA

Howard Lederer described John Juanda as "the greatest player in the world at adjusting to take advantage of conditions at the table." John does not have a single style—he's got lots of them. When the table conditions demand tight play, John can play tighter than Action Dan Harrington. When it's time to play loose, John can make Gus Hansen look timid.

"BIGGEST ONLINE WINNER"

There is a player—I'll call him the Biggest Online Winner, or BOW—who simply destroys the $25/$50 No Limit games on the Internet. I know his real name and screen name, but for his own protection I'm not going to divulge that information.

I've watched and played against him for hundreds of hours. He not only saps the chips, but the very spirit from the rocks in the game.

It would be an understatement to say that BOW

plays a very sound game. According to the branch of mathematics called game theory, his style is *unbeatable*. I've tried to emulate his cash-game style to some extent, although I haven't been nearly as successful with it as he has.

Here's the basic philosophy I've seen BOW employ:

1. Get in the pot cheaply.
2. Massively overbet with some premium draws.
3. Massively overbet with the nuts or the best hand.

For those who are more mathematically inclined, I offer a very detailed analysis of BOW's play in the following pages.

——BOW'S GAME THEORY——

Consider this example:

After the flop the pot is $500.
BOW has $5,000.
I have $5,000 and A♣ K♦.
The flop comes down: A♥ 7♠ 6♠
BOW moves all-in.

BOW Hand	Bet/Call	BOW Chances	His Pot Equity	My Chances	My Pot Equity
1 T♠8♠	$5,000	47.80%	$5,019	52.20%	$5,481
2 8♣5♥	$5,000	37.00%	$3,885	63.00%	$6,615
3 7♥7♦	$5,000	98.40%	$10,332	1.60%	$168
4 5♥9♣	$5,000	23.70%	$2,488	76.30%	$8,012
			$21,724		$20,276

Now, I *know* that BOW will be on a draw three quarters of the time he moves all-in. In scenario number four above, I'd be crazy not to call him—he's on a gut-shot straight draw for God's sake! I *have* to call with A-K. But doing so costs me dearly the one quarter of the time (like in scenario number three) that BOW has a monster and I'm drawing nearly dead.

By calling every time, I have no way to win long term. BOW's strategy will, eventually, take all of my money. He'll win $1,448 every four hands we play this way, or an average of $362 a hand.

Some other bonuses from his strategy:

♦ After he moves in on his opponents and they call with the best hand, BOW will often bust them with a draw, sending them into a chip-spewing suicide tilt. (Does it sound like I've been there before?)

♦ BOW will pick up a *ton* of chips from the pot when he doesn't get called. It is *very* difficult to pick up a hand you'd like to call the $5,000 bet with. For instance, a player with J-J will be "in the lead" in almost every scenario listed above but will be very hard-pressed to call all the chips with that ace on the board. By applying maximum pressure on his opponents, BOW picks up a lot of pots that he is not entitled to win just based on the strength of his hand.

The only real negative to his strategy that I can see is that he will suffer what mathematicians call "high variance," wild swings in his bankroll. He needs a very large bankroll to play this way. For example, if BOW moves all-in ten consecutive times with a 35% chance to win, he will miss all ten times about 1.5% of the time, a potential loss of $50,000. Given the amount of time he spends at the table, this should happen about once every few months.

The best way for me to counter BOW's strategy when I have the best hand is to get as much money as possible into the pot *before* the flop. Pushing even marginal advantages before the flop is vital to beating him.

Another strategy that will crush his play is to be more apt to call with a big draw than with a "made" hand. For instance, if I call his $5,000 bet with K♠ Q♠ against his four potential hands in the table above, my equity soars to more than $7,800!

Flop: A♥ 7♠ 6♠

I call the $5,000 bet with K♠ Q♠.

BOW Hand	Bet/Call	BOW Chances	His Pot Equity	My Chances	My Pot Equity
1 T♠8♠	$5,000	31.40%	$3,297	68.60%	$7,203
2 8♠5♥	$5,000	32.20%	$3,381	67.80%	$7,119
3 7♥7♦	$5,000	74.40%	$7,812	25.60%	$2,688
4 5♥9♠	$5,000	24.80%	$2,604	75.20%	$7,896
			$17,094		$24,906

As long as I have a better draw three out of four times when I call, and have a few outs those times he is ahead, I should be able to beat him. Of course, if BOW identifies the fact that I'm employing this strategy against him, he's very likely to change gears and start moving all-in with only the better hands. Ah, poker is a wonderful game.

While BOW's strategy crushes cash games, it's too volatile to work in tournaments. Survival is the primary concern when there are no rebuys allowed. To his immense credit, BOW does not employ this strategy in tournaments, where he is able to change gears and play a more tournament-savvy style of poker.

RULES OF NO LIMIT HOLD'EM

There is nothing here for an advanced player—or even a recreational one—but for the sake of completeness, here are the definitive rules of No Limit Hold'em.

THE BASICS

No Limit Texas Hold'em uses a standard fifty-two-card deck and can be played by two to twenty-three players. A disc (usually white plastic embossed with the word

"Dealer") known as the "button" designates which player is the dealer. This button rotates clockwise one seat after each hand. Before any of the fifty-two cards are dealt, however, the players must be offered a prize to fight for. The prize is called "the blinds." The player who sits immediately to the left of the dealer must post the "small blind" and the player immediately to the left of the small blind must post the "big blind." The small blind puts in a predetermined amount, let's say $10, and the big blind puts in what is usually double the amount of the small blind, in this case $20. In a cash game the size of the blinds at a given table—the "table stakes"—remains constant for each hand played. In a tournament the blinds increase at predetermined intervals. Each interval is called a "tournament level."

In most large tournaments antes are charged to each player once a certain level (usually the fourth or fifth) has been reached. The ante amount is generally about 25% of the big blind.

Once the blinds and antes have been put into the pot, two cards are dealt facedown to each player, one at a time. The deal begins with the player sitting to the left of the dealer and moves in a clockwise fashion until all players have their two "hole cards."

——PREFLOP BETTING——

Now the betting begins. The first round, or pre-flop betting, begins with the player sitting immediately to the left of the big blind, a position referred to as "under the gun."

The betting round is complete when each player has had his or her chance to fold, call, or raise. (Or in the case of the big blind—who has already posted a full bet—to check if the pot hasn't already been raised.)

——THE FLOP——

Now the dealer "burns" the top card, discarding it facedown and unseen on the table,* and deals the "flop": three cards faceup in the middle. These three cards, along with the two that will follow, are called "community cards" because they can be used by everyone who is still in the hand.

Another round of betting begins with the first player to the left of the dealer button who still has a live hand. This same order is followed for the remaining rounds.

---

*Burning a card discourages potential cheaters. If the top card were marked, players would know what card was coming next. This is more difficult after a burn card is dealt.

——THE TURN——

When the second round of betting is completed, the dealer burns another card and reveals the fourth community card, called "the turn" or "fourth street." A new round of betting ensues.

——THE RIVER——

Now the dealer burns one last card and reveals the final community card, called "the river" or "fifth street." There is a fourth and final round of betting that, once completed, leads to the showdown.

——THE SHOWDOWN——

The remaining players turn over their cards, beginning with the last player to bet or raise on the previous round of betting. If the next player's hand can beat or tie the first player's hand, then this player shows their cards. If their hand does not beat the first player's hand, they are not required to show their cards unless asked. The showdown continues until every hand has been turned over or discarded.

The winner is the one who can assemble the best

five-card hand out of the seven cards available—the five community cards and the individual player's two hole cards. A player can combine their hole and community cards in any combination, i.e., two cards from their hand and three cards from the board, one card from their hand and four cards from the board, or all five cards from the board.

——NO LIMIT BETTING——

What separates No Limit Texas Hold'em from Limit Texas Hold'em is the amount you can bet. In No Limit, as the name suggests, you can raise any or all of the amount you have in front of you at any time with one caveat: A raise must be at least the size of the previous bet or raise.

For example, if I bet $100, my opponent cannot then raise to $150, he must raise to at least $200, which is a $100 raise. The only exception to this rule comes in the case of an all-in bet, described below.

One key phrase in the description above is "in front of you." If you peek at your hole cards and see two aces winking back, don't start unloading cash from your wallet. You can only bet the amount that's in front of you on the table. The good news is, if you want to call a bet, you are only liable for covering it to the extent that you have chips in front of you. If someone bets more than you've got, you can simply go "all-in."

——ALL-IN——

A player bets $200. You only have $120. Does this mean you have to fold your hand?

Obviously not, or Bill Gates would be the most successful poker player on the planet. In this situation you can call the player's bet for the amount of the chips you have in front of you, in this case $120. You are said to be "all-in."

You can also go all-in to get around the minimum raising requirements. If you want to raise a player who has bet $500 but have only $700 in front of you, you are allowed to go all-in, calling the $500 and raising your remaining $200.

If an all-in pot is being contested by just two players, then the player with the bigger stack gets their excess chips returned to them, and the hand is played for the size of the smaller stack. However, if there are more than two people in the pot, a side pot must be created.

——SIDE POTS——

Side pots occur frequently in No Limit Hold'em. Let's say that there is $300 in the pot and then your opponent, we'll call him Bob, bets $200. You call Bob's bet by going all-in with your last $120. Another player, Alice, who has more than enough to cover Bob's bet, decides to call as well. It's time for the dealer to divide the chips into a main pot and a side pot.

The main pot will include the original $300 plus your $120, Bob's $120, and Alice's $120, for a total of $660. The excess $80 from each of the full bets posted by Bob and Alice will be placed into the side pot, which now contains $160. Any additional bets that Bob or Alice might make before the completion of the hand are also placed in the side pot.

You are only eligible, should you wind up with the best hand at the showdown, to win the main pot. The side pot will be won by Bob or Alice, whoever has the best hand between them. If either Bob or Alice has the best hand among the three of you, then he or she will win both the side pot and the main pot.

RULES OF ETIQUETTE

Whether you're playing in a casino or a home game, you should ask the floor manager or host if there are any "house rules" specific to the game.

You can find many of the most common rules of etiquette in Robert Ciaffone's outstanding rulebook, "Robert's Rules of Poker." He covers almost any situation that is likely to come up, from misdeals to "kill pots" to "straddle blinds."

Here are some key points of etiquette that are common to most games:

♣ Don't splash the pot.

Players "splash the pot" when they toss their chips directly into the pot. This is illegal because it makes it difficult for the dealer to verify the size of the bet. When adding chips to the pot, just place them directly in front of you. The dealer will count up your chips and then sweep them into the pot.

♣ Don't string bet.

A string bet occurs when a player reaches into his stack more than once while making a bet. If it were legal, a devious player could reach into his stack, place a bet, gauge his opponent's reaction, then reach back for more chips.

Many new players cost themselves the ability to raise by accidentally making string bets. To avoid doing so, you want to get into the habit of clearly saying "raise" when it's your turn to bet. A player who verbally declares a raise can reach back into his or her stack as many times as desired.

♣ Don't talk about the hand.

While your hand is in play, you may not announce what you have, either verbally or physically. Why would anyone do that? For the same reason someone would intentionally string bet: to gain information about an opponent's hand by gauging their reaction to your announcement.

♣ Don't intentionally act out of turn.

♣ Don't verbally agree to "check down" a hand with another player when a third opponent is all-in.

♣ Don't talk about the hand when you are not involved.

♣ Don't intentionally stall the game.

♣ Don't order someone to turn their cards faceup at the showdown.

You may *ask* someone to show their cards, but it is the dealer's job to *tell* them. Asking players to see their cards too frequently is considered bad etiquette.

♣ Don't mistreat the dealer!

    Remember that you're the one responsible for your actions at the poker table. Whatever the consequences—right, wrong, lucky, or unlucky—don't take it out on the dealer.

♣ Protect your hand from sneaky eyes when you peek at your hole cards.

♣ Keep your cards on the table at all times.

♣ Show both of your cards if required at the showdown.

♣ Protect your live hand. People use just about anything to protect their cards from accidentally being exposed. They place things such as lucky coins, trusty trinkets, or a lover's keepsake on the cards. I use a chip.

TOURNAMENT RULES AND PROCEDURES

For a complete list of rules and procedures pertaining to tournaments, check out the Poker Tournament Directors Association Web site:

www.pokertda.com

CHARTS AND TABLES

In the next few pages, I have provided some charts and tables I find useful. Your mileage may vary. I certainly don't believe that most of this information needs to be memorized, nor will I claim to know it all by heart. And remember that there are many factors other than numbers that go into creating a great poker player—if you could win by looking poker up in a matrix or a graph, computers would win every tournament and I'd be out of business.

STARTING HANDS

The following suggestions about what hands to play from various positions at the table are based on a few primary assumptions:

- ♥ I have a tight-aggressive image and the respect of the table.
- ♥ I am playing against average-strength opponents.
- ♥ I have an average stack and so do my opponents.
- ♥ I am the first player to voluntarily enter the pot.
- ♥ I am coming in for a raise anywhere from two-and-a-half to four times the size of the big blind.

Hands that appear in outlined text are hands that I would play from that position only about 25–50% of the time. I would almost always play the same hand from a later position.

Remember that these charts are just guidelines. Adjustments based on changing table conditions and your opponents' individual styles are vital to success at No Limit Hold'em.

Merely following these starting-hand charts is not enough to ensure winning.

All charts can be found in color, printable formats on my Web site:

www.philgordonpoker.com/littlegreenbook.html

—— AVERAGE GAME ——

Game: Average 2–3 players max before the flop
(not tight, not loose)

Action: First to the pot, and raising

Players: 9- to 10-handed

Suited Hands

AA	AK	AQ	AJ	AT	A9	A8	A7	A6	A5	A4	A3	A2
AK	KK	KQ	KJ	KT	K9	K8	K7	K6	K5	K4	K3	K2
AQ	KQ	QQ	QJ	QT	Q9	Q8	Q7	Q6	Q5	Q4	Q3	Q2
AJ	KJ	QJ	JJ	JT	J9	J8	J7	J6	J5	J4	J3	J2
AT	KT	QT	JT	TT	T9	T8	T7	T6	T5	T4	T3	T2
A9	K9	Q9	J9	T9	99	98	97	96	95	94	93	92
A8	K8	Q8	J8	T8	98	88	87	86	85	84	83	82
A7	K7	Q7	J7	T7	97	87	77	76	75	74	73	72
A6	K6	Q6	J6	T6	96	86	76	66	65	64	63	62
A5	K5	Q5	J5	T5	95	85	75	65	55	54	53	52
A4	K4	Q4	J4	T4	94	84	74	64	54	44	43	42
A3	K3	Q3	J3	T3	93	83	73	63	53	43	33	32
A2	K2	Q2	J2	T2	92	82	72	62	52	42	32	22

Unsuited Hands

262

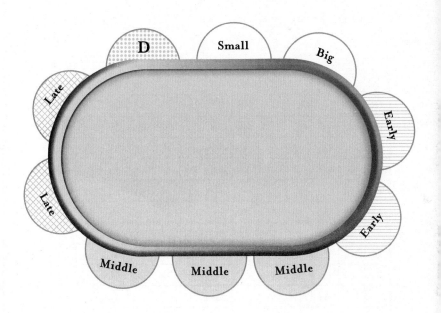

—I'M PLAYING TIGHT—

Game: Average 3–5 players before the flop

Action: First to the pot, and raising

Players: 9- to 10-handed

Suited Hands

AA	AK	AQ	AJ	AT	A9	A8	A7	A6	A5	A4	A3	A2
AK	KK	KQ	KJ	KT	K9	K8	K7	K6	K5	K4	K3	K2
AQ	KQ	QQ	QJ	QT	Q9	Q8	Q7	Q6	Q5	Q4	Q3	Q2
AJ	KJ	QJ	JJ	JT	J9	J8	J7	J6	J5	J4	J3	J2
AT	KT	QT	JT	TT	T9	T8	T7	T6	T5	T4	T3	T2
A9	K9	Q9	J9	T9	99	98	97	96	95	94	93	92
A8	K8	Q8	J8	T8	98	88	87	86	85	84	83	82
A7	K7	Q7	J7	T7	97	87	77	76	75	74	73	72
A6	K6	Q6	J6	T6	96	86	76	66	65	64	63	62
A5	K5	Q5	J5	T5	95	85	75	65	55	54	53	52
A4	K4	Q4	J4	T4	94	84	74	64	54	44	43	42
A3	K3	Q3	J3	T3	93	83	73	63	53	43	33	32
A2	K2	Q2	J2	T2	92	82	72	62	52	42	32	22

Unsuited Hands

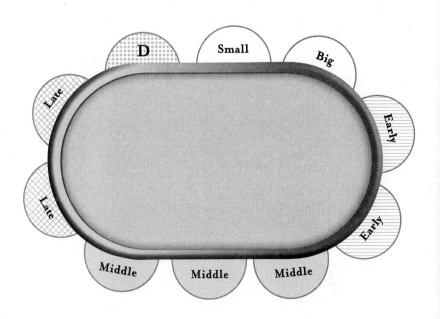

Game: Average 2 players before the flop
Action: First to the pot, and raising
Players: 9- to 10-handed

Suited Hands

AA	AK	AQ	AJ	AT	A9	A8	A7	A6	A5	A4	A3	A2
AK	KK	KQ	KJ	KT	K9	K8	K7	K6	K5	K4	K3	K2
AQ	KQ	QQ	QJ	QT	Q9	Q8	Q7	Q6	Q5	Q4	Q3	Q2
AJ	KJ	QJ	JJ	JT	J9	J8	J7	J6	J5	J4	J3	J2
AT	KT	QT	JT	TT	T9	T8	T7	T6	T5	T4	T3	T2
A9	K9	Q9	J9	T9	99	98	97	96	95	94	93	92
A8	K8	Q8	J8	T8	98	88	87	86	85	84	83	82
A7	K7	Q7	J7	T7	97	87	77	76	75	74	73	72
A6	K6	Q6	J6	T6	96	86	76	66	65	64	63	62
A5	K5	Q5	J5	T5	95	85	75	65	55	54	53	52
A4	K4	Q4	J4	T4	94	84	74	64	54	44	43	42
A3	K3	Q3	J3	T3	93	83	73	63	53	43	33	32
A2	K2	Q2	J2	T2	92	82	72	62	52	42	32	22

Unsuited Hands

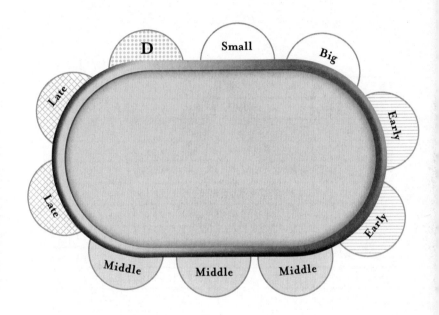

267

——SHORTHANDED, AVERAGE——

Game: Average 2 players before the flop
Action: First to the pot, and raising
Players: 5- to 6-handed

Suited Hands

AA	AK	AQ	AJ	AT	A9	A8	A7	A6	A5	A4	A3	A2
AK	KK	KQ	KJ	KT	K9	K8	K7	K6	K5	K4	K3	K2
AQ	KQ	QQ	QJ	QT	Q9	Q8	Q7	Q6	Q5	Q4	Q3	Q2
AJ	KJ	QJ	JJ	JT	J9	J8	J7	J6	J5	J4	J3	J2
AT	KT	QT	JT	TT	T9	T8	T7	T6	T5	T4	T3	T2
A9	K9	Q9	J9	T9	99	98	97	96	95	94	93	92
A8	K8	Q8	J8	T8	98	88	87	86	85	84	83	82
A7	K7	Q7	J7	T7	97	87	77	76	75	74	73	72
A6	K6	Q6	J6	T6	96	86	76	66	65	64	63	62
A5	K5	Q5	J5	T5	95	85	75	65	55	54	53	52
A4	K4	Q4	J4	T4	94	84	74	64	54	44	43	42
A3	K3	Q3	J3	T3	93	83	73	63	53	43	33	32
A2	K2	Q2	J2	T2	92	82	72	62	52	42	32	22

Unsuited Hands

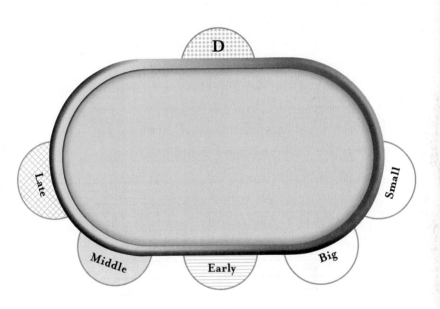

OUTS

I use this chart to figure out the chances of winning after the flop and the turn. The Rules of Four and Two (see page 178) provide close approximations, but here are the exact values.

Note that the postflop column does not contain any adjustment for opponents' redraws, i.e., those times they pick up a backdoor flush or straight. This table assumes that if I hit my hand, it will be a winner.

	Postflop		Postturn	
Outs	Rules of 4	Exact	Rule of 2	Exact
1	4	4.5%	2	2.3%
2	8	8.8%	4	4.5%
3	12	13.0%	6	6.8%
4	16	17.2%	8	9.1%
5	20	21.2%	10	11.4%
6	24	25.2%	12	13.6%
7	28	29.0%	14	15.9%
8	32	32.7%	16	18.2%
9	36	36.4%	18	20.5%
10	40	39.9%	20	22.7%
11	44	43.3%	22	25.0%
12	48	46.7%	24	27.3%
13	52	49.9%	26	29.5%
14	56	53.0%	28	31.8%
15	60	56.1%	30	34.1%
16	64	59.0%	32	36.4%
17	68	61.8%	34	38.6%

PREFLOP CHANCES

The chances of being dealt . . .

A-A	0.45%
A-A or K-K	0.90%
Any pocket pair	5.90%
A-K suited	0.30%
A-K offsuit	0.90%
Any A-K	1.20%
A-A, K-K, any A-K	2.10%
Two suited cards	24.00%

If I have a pocket pair, I will flop . . .

A set	10.80%
A full house	0.70%
Four of a kind	0.20%
Set or better	11.80%

If I am suited, I will . . .

Flop a flush	0.84%
Flop a flush draw	10.90%
Flop a three-card flush	41.60%
	(need two more!)
Make flush by river	6.40%

If I am unpaired in the hole, I will flop . . .

At least one pair	32.40%
Exactly one pair	29.00%
	(using one hole card)
Two pair	2.00%
	(using both hole cards)
Trips	1.35%
Full house	0.10%
Quads	0.01%
	(dream on)

When the flop comes down, it will be . . .

Trips	0.24%
Paired	17.00%
Suited	5.20%
Rainbow (three suits)	40.00%
Sequenced (4-5-6)	3.50%
Two sequence (K-5-6)	40.00%
Unsequenced (2-5-Q)	56.00%

On the turn, I'll make a . . .

Full house or better after flopping a set (seven outs)	15%
Full house after flopping two pair (four outs)	9%

Flush after flopping a four flush (nine outs)	19%
Straight after flopping two-way draw (eight outs)	17%
Straight after flopping a gut-shot (four outs)	9%
Pair after flopping two overcards (six outs)	13%

After the flop, if I go to the river, I'll make a . . .

Full house or better after flopping a set	33%
Full house or better after flopping two pair	17%
Flush after flopping a four flush	35%
Backdoor (runner-runner) flush	4.2%
Straight after flopping two-way draw	32%
Straight after flopping a gut-shot	17%
Pair or better after flopping two overcards	24%

With just the river to come, I'll make a . . .

Full house or better with a set (ten outs)	23%
Full house out of two pair (four outs)	9.1%
Flush from a four flush (nine outs)	20%
Straight with two-ways to make it (eight outs)	17%
Gut-shot straight (four outs)	8%
Pair with two overcards (six outs)	13%

HAND RANKINGS

(No poker book would be complete without one.)

Royal Flush
A-K-Q-J-T, all of the same suit
A♠ K♠ Q♠ J♠ T♠

Straight Flush
Five cards in a sequence, all the same suit
(ace can be low or high)
6♠ 7♠ 8♠ 9♠ T♠
A♥ 2♥ 3♥ 4♥ 5♥

Four of a Kind
Four cards of the same rank
J♥ J♣ J♦ J♠ 8♦

Full House
Three of a kind and a pair
7♥ 7♠ 7♦ T♣ T♥
K♦ K♥ K♠ 2♣ 2♠

Flush
Five cards of the same suit

A♣ 9♣ 6♣ 5♣ 2♣

K♥ Q♥ T♥ 9♥ 4♥

Straight
Five cards in a sequence

4♥ 5♥ 6♠ 7♦ 8♣

Three of a Kind
Three cards of the same rank

4♥ 4♠ 4♦ A♣ Q♦

Two Pair
Two cards of one rank, two cards of a different rank

A♣ A♦ J♥ J♠ 4♣

One Pair
Two cards of the same rank

6♠ 6♦ 9♥ 4♦ 2♣

No Pair (High Card)

A♥ J♦ T♣ 9♦ 5♣

WSOP TOURNAMENT STRUCTURE

Level	Small	Big	Ante
1	25	50	0
2	50	100	0
3	100	200	0
4	100	200	25
5	150	300	50
6	200	400	50
7	250	500	50
8	300	600	75
9	400	800	100
10	500	1,000	100
11	600	1,200	200
12	800	1,600	200
13	1,000	2,000	300
14	1,200	2,400	400
15	1,500	3,000	500
16	2,000	4,000	500
17	2,500	5,000	500
18	3,000	6,000	1,000
19	4,000	8,000	1,000
20	5,000	10,000	1,000
21	6,000	12,000	2,000
22	8,000	16,000	2,000
23	10,000	20,000	3,000
24	12,000	24,000	4,000
25	15,000	30,000	5,000
26	20,000	40,000	5,000
27	25,000	50,000	5,000

Each level lasts two hours.

All players start with $10,000 in tournament chips.

FULLTILTPOKER.COM
SIT & GO TOURNAMENT
STRUCTURE

Level	Small	Big
1	10	20
2	15	30
3	20	40
4	25	50
5	30	60
6	40	80
7	50	100
8	60	120
9	80	160
10	100	200
11	120	240
12	150	300
13	200	400
14	250	500
15	300	600
16	400	800
17	500	1,000
18	600	1,200

Each level lasts six minutes.

All players start with $1,500 in tournament chips.

(Note: Six minutes of Internet play is approximately equal to twenty minutes of casino play.)

FURTHER STUDY

There are many books and other sources of information that have improved my play. I have read and reread all of them and will forever be thankful to the authors for helping me become a better player.

BOOKS

The Theory of Poker
By David Sklansky
Two Plus Two Publications

Hold'em Poker for Advanced Players
By David Sklansky and Mason Malmuth
Two Plus Two Publications

Tournament Poker for Advanced Players
By David Sklansky
Two Plus Two Publications

Caro's Book of Poker Tells:The Pyschology and Body Language of Poker
By Mike Caro
Cardoza Publishing

Doyle Brunson's Super System: A Course in Power Poker
By Doyle Brunson
Cardoza Publishing

Doyle Brunson's Super System 2: A Course in Power Poker
By Doyle Brunson
Cardoza Publishing

Championship No-Limit & Pot-Limit Hold'em
By T. J. Cloutier and Tom McEvoy
Cardoza Publishing

Harrington on Hold'em: Expert Strategy for No Limit Tournaments
By Dan Harrington
Two Plus Two Publications

The Art of War
Sun Tzu
Running Press Book Publishers

PERIODICALS

Bluff
www.bluffmagazine.com

Card Player Magazine
www.cardplayer.com

All In
www.allinmagazine.com

WEB SITES

Phil Gordon's Home Page
www. philgordonpoker.com

Full Tilt Poker
www.fulltiltpoker.com

ESPN Poker Club
http://sports.espn.go.com/espn/poker/

Poker Stove: A Poker Odds Calculator
www.pokerstove.com

Two Plus Two Forums (for poker discussion)
www.twoplustwo.com

The rec.gambling.poker Newsgroup
www.recpoker.com
(or any newsgroup reader)

Home Poker Games
www.homepokergames.com

The (Unofficial) *World Poker Tour* Fan Site
www.wptfan.com

Matt Savage's Tournament Director Site
www.savagetournaments.com

The Tiltboys' Home Page
www.tiltboys.com

SHAMELESS PLUGS

And now, some shameless plugs for my other works:

Poker: The Real Deal
By Phil Gordon and Jonathan Grotenstein
Simon Spotlight Entertainment

Expert Insight: Final Table Poker with Phil Gordon
DVD Series
By Phil Gordon
www.expertinsight.com

Tales from the Tiltboys
By the Tiltboys
Edited by Kim Scheinberg
Foreword by Phil Gordon
Sports Publishing, Inc.

AFTERWORD

Writing this book was a daunting task for me, but a task worth completing. I am immensely proud of what I've been able to accomplish. Throughout the process, I used the act of writing to explore my own game and the games of the players I admire. Along the way I've learned quite a few things about my own play that will, I hope, make me better.

When I started this book, I didn't think there would be so much math. Forgive me if it was overwhelming. What I've come to realize, however, is that I rely on mathematics at the table far more often than I'd thought.

And if this book is about anything, it's about the way I make decisions at the poker table. If people browsing in the store pick it up, see a bunch of math, graphs, and charts and are turned off, so be it. I couldn't write my complete thoughts on the game without including these things. I'm choosing completeness over sales.

If some of the concepts in this book make you a better player, I am thrilled. If you disagree with some of what I've written, *you may very well be right*. As I've said all along, there is more than one way to win. I've presented here, to the best of my ability, the way I play. Play your own game and style.

With a little bit of luck and a whole lot of heart, I hope to meet you at the final table of a big tournament, the piles of cash on the table, the TV cameras rolling. I'll be sitting on my *Little Green Book*, hoping that I can play the game at a level that does justice to what I've written and to the game I love.

Over time I am sure that people will find errors in this text. I'm sure that I'll think of things that I forgot to include. Unfortunately, the book business doesn't allow rebuys, add-ons, or instant reprints. Instead I'll rely on the Internet. Please join me on my Web site at the address below for corrections, updates, and new thoughts. The *Little Green Book* is a living, growing document that I will be updating as often as possible. If you have something to share, please send it to me for inclusion. Together we'll keep exploring the game, refining thoughts, and working to better understand No Limit Hold'em.

No Limit Texas Hold'em takes just a minute to learn, and a lifetime to master. Indeed.

Good luck. I'm all-in.

Phil Gordon
June 1, 2005

Phil Gordon's Little Green Book Web site:

www.philgordonpoker.com/littlegreenbook.html

Great poker players are not made overnight and reading a book on poker strategy will not guarantee your success, much less make you an instant contender for the *World Series of Poker*'s final table. My hope is that this book will help you think more critically about how to play No Limit Hold'em, so please don't treat this book as an instruction manual or definitive guide. The best players develop their own style and methods, and there is no system that will work for everyone.

PHIL GORDON is the cohost of *Celebrity Poker Showdown*, a world-class poker player, and the author of *Poker: The Real Deal*. He has won more than $1.2 million in tournament purses in the past three years, including two wins on the *World Poker Tour* and a fourth-place finish in the *World Series of Poker* championship event. He lives in Las Vegas.